AMERICAN ELEGY

AMERICAN ELEGY

ELEGY

✦

A Family Memoir

Jeffrey Simpson

A DUTTON BOOK

DUTTON
Published by the Penguin Group
Penguin Books USA Inc., 375 Hudson Street, New York, New York 10014, U.S.A.
Penguin Books Ltd, 27 Wrights Lane, London W8 5TZ, England
Penguin Books Australia Ltd, Ringwood, Victoria, Australia
Penguin Books Canada Ltd, 10 Alcorn Avenue,
Toronto, Ontario, Canada M4V 3B2
Penguin Books (N.Z.) Ltd, 182–190 Wairau Road, Auckland 10, New Zealand

Penguin Books Ltd, Registered Offices: Harmondsworth, Middlesex, England

First published by Dutton, an imprint of Dutton Signet,
a division of Penguin Books USA Inc.
Distributed in Canada by McClelland & Stewart Inc.

First Printing, September, 1996
10 9 8 7 6 5 4 3 2 1

 REGISTERED TRADEMARK — MARCA REGISTRADA

LIBRARY OF CONGRESS CATALOGING-IN-PUBLICATION DATA:

Simpson, Jeffrey.
   American elegy : a family memoir / Jeffrey Simpson.
      p.   cm.
   ISBN 0-525-94122-3
   1. Simpson, Jeffrey—Family. 2. Simpson family. 3. Parnassus (Pa.)—Biography.
4. City and town life—Pennsylvania—Parnassus.
I. Title.
F159.P24S56   1996   96-17109
974.8'81—dc20   CIP

Printed in the United States of America
Set in Goudy
Designed by Eve L. Kirch

This book is printed on acid-free paper. ∞

To Peg

Contents

Part Three ★ Lucille and Chauncey

Part Four ★ Getting Away

Part Five ★ The Flood

Part Six ★ Postlude

Author's Note

When I began to write down these stories many years ago, the people in the generation or two before me who had told them to me were still alive. To free myself—and to give them freedom from my interpretations—I changed the names in those generations. I have left the people in the book with those borrowed names. In the generations farther back the names are historically verifiable. All of the documents referred to exist.

Part One

TOWN AND COUNTRY

THE AMAZONS

In 1792 on the banks of the Kiskiminetas River in Western
Pennsylvania there lived a woman named Mary Harbison, known as
Massy. Now there was a great deal of trouble with the Indians in
those days in that newly settled land, and the settlers only returned to
their cabins in the spring after spending the winter in the fort. Early
one morning when Massy Harbison went to the spring for water—the
leaves all feathery green around her and the swamp lilies crunching
underfoot—she heard bleating sorts of cries, like those of a lamb, and
hastened back to the cabin because there were surely no lambs in the
forest and the cry might be a sign from savage to savage. Then there
came a morning when her husband had gone to the fort nearby and
left the plank door of the cabin open so that the sun, burning off the
mist, spread a curtain of speckled gold across the doorway and
warmed the dirt floor of the cabin. Massy Harbison, lying in bed
nursing her youngest child, fell asleep with the babe at her breast. She
was wakened by savages—brown muscular men with impassive faces
and the nervous eyes of forest animals—who pulled her by the feet
from the bed the way she pulled the cow in from the pasture.

She clutched her babe to her bosom, she wrestled them to get a
petticoat to wear over her shift, all to no avail. She watched a
neighbor shot dead as he approached the gate of the fort across the
meadow; she saw her second son, a lad of three years, murdered, his

brains dashed out against the doorpost of the cabin. She was driven by
the Indians, Senecas they were and Munsies—although two of the
number were white men, renegades, painted as savages—across the
countryside to the great Allegheny River. Holding her babe while her
other little boy was carried by one of the Indians, she was taken across
the water in one of the canoes that the warriors had hidden in reeds
along the bank. When they had crossed, the savage who had her older
boy in hand felled him with his tomahawk and scalped him before his
mother's eyes. She sank senseless, was brought to by blows, and
seeing the scrap of bloody skin and brown hair soaked black in blood,
sank senseless again, whereupon the savages threw the scalp away
and led Massy into the water. They dunked her, still holding her
youngest babe, and the cries of the child recalled her to her senses.

Three days later at dawn, as her guard slept, Massy stole away
from camp. She and her babe were guided to the river by a flock of
robins, which miraculously appeared in the sky above a clearing.

She hailed three white men on the far riverbank, and when one
dared to approach in a canoe she recognized him as her neighbor, but
he demanded, "Who in the Name of God are you?" so changed was
she in a matter of days by her tribulation.

She was rescued with her infant still at her breast, and at the fort at
Pittsburgh, where she was taken, 150 thorns as counted by one Felix
Nigley were plucked from her feet.

A year later Massy Harbison and her husband settled on Puckety
Creek in the same neighborhood and she bore six children more. She
lived to a venerated old age.

—ADAPTATION OF AN ACCOUNT TAKEN FROM
A HISTORY OF THE COUNTY OF WESTMORELAND, PENNSYLVANIA
BY GEORGE G. ALBERT, 1882.

By blood the land was bought. Sacrifices were required, and
in an Old Testament way there were offerings of life and
flesh before the salvation of freedom on your own land could be
attained. Stories such as that of Massy Harbison were epic: two

children slaughtered before a mother's eyes; six days and nights wandering in the wilderness. The early tales became decorated with the details of myth—the cries of false lambs in the forest; the miraculous flock of robins showing the mother, her babe at the breast, the way back to the river of life.

The land was achieved by blood.

Then it was consecrated to hope. Aspiration was the watchword of the early place names. They aspired to righteousness—Unity, Congruity—or to the heroic—Washington, Jefferson—or to classical perfection—Apollo, Tarentum, Sardis—and Parnassus.

> **Par•nas´sus** (pär•näs´ŭs). 1. Former borough, Westmoreland co., SW Pennsylvania, on Allegheny river ab. 17 m. ENE of Pittsburgh; pop. (1930) 6240; consolidated with New Kensington (q.v.) 1931.
> —Webster's Geographical Dictionary, 1969

When my grandfather died he was living on a third of an acre that was the only piece remaining from a three-hundred-acre land grant his great-great-grandfather received for playing the fife in the Revolutionary War. The grant was near the town of Parnassus, Pennsylvania.

Parnassus had been a railroad town and the county market town. It had ceased to exist—as Webster's duly noted—in 1931 when it had been absorbed into the neighboring mill town of New Kensington. I was born posthumously to the culture I sprang from. The pageant that I had seen as I was growing up, the church bazaars, choir practice, bridge club, were what was left of an old organic society: the farming community of Western Pennsylvania as it had been settled in the eighteenth century by the Northern Irish Protestants, known as Scotch-Irish, and the Rhineland Germans, who had first settled near Philadelphia and were known as Pennsylvania Dutch. After coal and gas were discovered in those Allegheny Mountain foothills, and the mills in the 1880s made Pittsburgh the industrial center of the world, the remaining Anglo-Saxon farming families continued to live in a ritualized way that paid homage to their small-town roots. But it had become a hollow ritual. There was less heart and less reason to their lives. The Janus God, dour to the Presbyterians for whom hellfire lurked around the edges of life like a forest fire nibbling the border of a plowed field and benign to the Germans who brought a tradition of Rhenish well-being to the New World, this God who had ordered every movement of life, the seedtime and harvest of the heart and the marriage bed, became more and more remote a figure. He became private, an object of devotion, whereas before He had been a Giver of the Law. The hill farms, where only one level field had sustained families for 150 years, gave out, and the men turned to keeping books in the mills, the women turned to teaching school.

Somewhere, I knew only too well, those families lost their sense of purpose. The urge and opportunities they sensed and followed from Ulster and the Palatinate to the backwoods of Pennsylvania in the 1770s, the perseverance they showed as they hewed farms and held them in the wilderness, all the strength became rigidity and resignation. Character that allowed the stoic bearing and burial of children ravaged by Indians and disease spat itself out in domestic rages—which sister got Mama's good china, who ate the last potato in the dish—or became flaccid in the latter generations. The men took jobs that presented themselves—they were not Horatio Algers, although they lived at the center of a burgeoning mill economy—and sank into apathy; the women held families, growing older, always more contrary, together. They were no longer builders but custodians of a culture.

Parnassus survived like one of those Victorian mantel ornaments under a glass dome. Faded, with no remnant of scent and only the memory of color, the form of the flowers stays perfect as long as the dome is not lifted and no air touches the arrangement.

Within a two-year span my old-maid aunts and my grandfather and stepgrandmother—my father's sisters and my mother's parents, the senior members of my whole family—died. My parents had moved to a suburb of Pittsburgh years before, so suddenly there was no Parnassus. The dome had been lifted. The Parnassus Presbyterian Church, white, wood-Gothic, surrounded by decaying elms, the church where Aunt Charlotte had sung in the choir for sixty-eight years and where Lucius Quintus Dinsmore, my grandfather, had been a member of the governing session for fifty years, joined forces with two neighboring churches because of declining membership. There was scarcely a trace of the town left.

What remained for me were two hundred years of letters, diaries, farm receipts, snapshots, daguerreotypes, account books, and newspaper clippings. The families had left records of their daily concerns for two hundred years. It made a map of the feelings, values, and progress of America during those years. And feelings, I was coming to believe, did not change.

As I came back to New York after the fourth funeral in little more than a year, I thought of those proud, cranky, kind old ladies and the more shadowy men, and I thought of the sepia images I had of them in their youth, and the stories of lives beyond those, and I thought of the stories in the trunkloads of papers and sticks of furniture, and I decided that I would trace them back to the Eden that never was.

I will begin with an image they would have hated.

A young couple who lived across the street from me in New York City when I was young made love at night with their bedroom curtains open. Night after night, in their high brownstone bedroom, the two forms twined and separated, twisting together and falling open like a cable of thick white hemp coming apart. Their window was directly across from mine, and although their light was not high, it was quite adequate to illuminate them. And night after night I looked at them. I do not think of myself as a voyeur. I did not look at them for very long.

They were like figures on an old Japanese tray that my aunts once gave me. They were shapely but distant enough from me to look at once solid and soft. The edges of their white bodies were blurred and there were no marring details of wrinkles or pimples, nor any enhancing details like pretty eyes or strong teeth. He had brown hair in thick, rather pointed locks; she had blond hair of a particularly yellow corn color. That is all I know.

Sometimes they just lay on the bed. They must have been talking or watching television—there was a blue emanation from one corner of the room like a ghostly presence that seemed to fix their attention. But I could not see the television and their lying so casually nude and easing in and out of physical contact with each other (she would nestle against him, he would calmly slap her rear, provoking no reaction) made them seem like Adam and Eve. They were all innocence, all natural.

Then, one night—it was in the late fall and the sparse city leaves had come off the trees—I noticed that they were lying on their bed in dressing gowns. His was a thick cream color that made his skin look faintly gold by comparison; hers was a deep red of some silky material that clung and defined the curves of her body. This was unusual—their being clothed—and I contin-ued to watch. He leaped up suddenly from the bed and left the room as though he were answering a summons. Which, in fact, he was. In a minute or so a lanky man with a black beard, wear-ing a rough blue shirt and jeans, walked into the bedroom. He sat down on the edge of the bed and the girl in the red dressing gown leaned over and kissed him. The visitor was animated and talked, waving his hands and twisting around to look at the television corner.

I felt an odd excitement. The entrance of the man and the couple's clothes suddenly transposed the scene from Arcadia to the drawing room. Suddenly there was society. There was the possibility of complications and conversations and stories. Much more was happening—or something qualitatively different—than the private, sensual world I had seen before.

I was intrigued. Ever since I had been a small boy in Western Pennsylvania I had witnessed other people's lives through what seemed to be a pane of glass. Because I was an only child I had heard stories from the aunts and my grandparents about people who were much older than I—or even dead—and the live ones

turned up briefly in cameo appearances where their slightest ut-
terance was weighty because of the history I knew about them.
As an adult, working as a journalist, I continued to observe and
piece together bits and fragments of lives.

Later in the autumn I saw the man with the beard visiting
across the street more often. Sometimes he and the blond girl
were together; sometimes all three of them. Then one evening I
noticed the couple, nude on their bed as usual, but lying two feet
apart. He had his arms crossed on his chest and his chin sunk;
the girl was busily doing some small futile action with her hands.
Something caught their attention, because she looked up inquir-
ingly and he warily. Neither moved. Then she spoke to him, he
shrugged, she spoke again. I looked down into the street and,
moving along the sidewalk beneath the web of tree branches like
a fish swimming in the expanse of a net, there was the man with
the beard. The man in the bedroom had refused to answer the
buzzer.

After that I was busy with my own concerns for a time and I
put the people across the street into the back of my mind. From
time to time when I did look over, I saw that the curtains were
unaccustomedly closed.

It was about that time that one of my two old-maid aunts, May
Kincaid, died. She had lived for eighty years in a state of belligerent civility with her sister Charlotte, also unmarried, who had
died the year before. As I had for Aunt Charlotte, I went home
for Aunt May's funeral.

Aunt May had been a commanding, handsome woman with
snow white hair and black eyebrows who wore plain dresses with
broad white collars so that she looked like a Protestant nun. She
liked to think of herself as meek, although in fact she was willful
and contentious. She had carried on a forty-year friendship with
back-slapping, glad-handing Jack Love (whom she worked for as
manager of the Keystone Dairy office) while she remained a pillar
of the church and ostracized friends from her small-town society
for actually doing far less than it appeared she was doing with
Jack Love. Several times during the course of their friendship

Jack Love married and was divorced, but May stuck. They went shopping twice a week, she stopped at his house every afternoon for several hours, and she filled out his income-tax forms for him each year. Given to quoting such poems as "Truth forever on the scaffold . . . ," her private thoughts may have been: "My strength is as the strength of ten because my heart is pure, and let people think what low thoughts they will."

As far as low thoughts went, my mother and stepgrandmother were always convinced May was having an affair, although they would never have actually said so. Instead, my stepgrandmother would say doubtfully, meaning the opposite, "I *know* May is a good girl."

Whatever the truth, May's legend went into the grave with her except for one jarring note. At her funeral I was standing beside my elderly cousin Ella, a monumental woman with sad, resigned eyes and black hair streaked with white. "It's remarkable that May never allowed herself to marry Jack Love," I said. And Ella answered in her high voice, oddly thin coming from such a massive presence, "I don't think she had any choice. I always heard *he* wouldn't marry *her*."

This was a startling departure from the notion of May as the bastion of order and morality, holding herself aloof from Jack. But I did not have time to think a great deal more about it then and I returned to New York.

Later, in the frail white glow of April Saturday sunlight, I turned the corner near my apartment from Eleventh Street onto Sixth Avenue, and I saw coming toward me the bearded man who visited across the street and the blond woman who lived there. I hadn't seen or thought about them for months. First I looked at the blond woman and saw that she looked much older than I had thought; there were circles under her eyes and she was very pale. The man was talking. I looked again at the woman. She had a look of total concentration and watched the man as though that gaze was all that was holding her on earth. But he was looking straight ahead and was oblivious. Whatever he was talking about had little to do with her. Her obsessed look, unrequited, shot through me and removed time, putting me in another place and another moment.

I remembered, years before when I had been a child, one of the few times I was permitted to see Jack Love, of whom the rest of the family didn't approve. He had come into May and her sister Charlotte's house on Fifth Avenue in Parnassus, overcoat flapping, face like a ripe tomato, and he had boomed, bending over to take my hand, "Well, fella, how are you?" He said something to everybody else in the room, but he never said anything particular to May, and I very distinctly remembered (because usually she was completely available to me, an indulged only nephew) that her attention was turned to him, like a flashlight shining on him wherever he moved.

I remembered further that in May's house the telephone was likely to ring at any hour of day or night and that you never made any comment on it. She would move slowly but inexorably away from a Sunday dinner table surrounded by her guests to answer the shrilling old-fashioned column telephone that stood on a stand in the hall. Or, staying overnight, I would hear the phone beside May's bed ring at four or six in the morning. When she talked in the hall, what you could hear of her voice had a cajoling, tentative quality quite unlike her usual infallible pronouncements of "We do not play cards on Sunday" (with a tinge of sorrow for those so benighted that they did) or "Well, she wasn't a *bad* person, but . . ." Her voice, when she talked to Jack Love, seemed to be always trying to find out what he wanted to say—with no thought of herself.

The look of the woman toward her companion on Sixth Avenue had brought May's look toward Jack Love in front of me, and I saw, in a sort of double vision, the look and what it meant at the same time. I remembered his inattentive acceptance of her as though she were a warm coat or a good book or a mother. I understood then that Ella was right, and the reason May never married Jack Love was that Jack Love would never marry May.

Shortly after May's death, my grandfather died, and then my stepgrandmother, and the Parnassus houses were closed up. But I continued to think about those people in Pennsylvania. The transparency of the private life across the street from me and the complication a third person introduced suggested whole gulfs that I had only suspected between the private feelings and public lives of those Olympians I had grown up among.

THE AUNTS

W HEN they died in the 1970s, Aunt Charlotte and Aunt
May had never owned or driven a car, they had never
owned a washing machine, and their lives were circumscribed
by ritual and order. Colored Hallie came on Monday and
Wednesday, choir practice and bridge club took place on
Thursday and Friday, Horne's Department Store automatically
sent out their winter coats in the fall and picked them up in the
spring. Their household had a regimental division of duties:
Charlotte kept house—that is, directed Hallie and packed the
laundry for the Polish washwoman—while May cooked. So
strictly separated were the territories, in fact, that Charlotte
could not cook anything for herself except oatmeal in the
morning, which May wouldn't eat.

Charlotte was the bane of May's existence. When they were
girls their mother had died after two other sisters were married,
leaving a little brother, my father, at home. Shortly afterwards,
their father, broken by grief, some said ("irresponsible," snorted
Ruby, my stepgrandmother), left for California and never came
back. Charlotte, the oldest and a lean, anxious old maid from
girlhood, determined to keep the family together. She worked as
a clerk at McQuaide's Hardware Store, and then as a bookkeeper
at the tin mill and eventually in the great big offices of the

aluminum company. She fussed a lot and talked so much and so fast that my father took to calling her "Dutch" because you couldn't understand half of what she said.

She also determined to keep the family's place as "nice people" in Parnassus Society. ("Not much Society at present," she would write in letters to me when she was old.) So when Russell McAlistair, the doctor's son, invited my father to his twelfth birthday party, Charlotte bought my father his first long pants and made him, sulky with his hair plastered flat against his skull, attend.

She intended to see May through high school graduation, which she did, and then to see that she behaved herself. May took a position as a bookkeeper at the dairy store. Once, when a nice traveling man who came to the dairy company every few months selling paper supplies asked May to have supper with him at the Howard Hotel and to see *Birth of a Nation*, Charlotte went along on the date.

May was pretty bitter about that. "She used to go with me when I was asked *out*," she would say years later. "She never leaves me alone for a minute. I have no life of my own at all." "Well, move out," my father would bark, but somehow that never happened.

By middle age Charlotte and May were inseparable, but then May had become the dominant front-line figure. She manipulated most of her family and half the town with imperturbable soft-spoken grace. She was, for one thing, always late. She was late to church, half a block away. "Here comes May, church can start now," Emerson McSparren, the head usher, would chuckle to the other gentlemen standing at the door. She was late to my parents' wedding ("She never wanted your father to get married," my mother would mutter darkly). And when they entertained— always at May's invitation—Charlotte would meet the guests at the door, and only after everyone was seated in the living room and general conversation had commenced would May come slowly down the stairs into the big front hall and appear in the back of the room. Though she would have claimed she didn't want anyone to take special notice, of course all the gentlemen had to stand up and all of the ladies had to greet their hostess.

Two of the people who often attended May's evening parties—sometimes for dinner and general conversation, sometimes for bridge and supper later—were Rutherford Park and his wife, Lillian. Rutherford was a little, bald, quick-spoken gentleman who had been my father's best friend all through their days at Parnassus High School together. He was a banker, although Father always said he didn't see how Ruddy made his balance sheets come out right; he was so notionate that he might just take it into his head someday that two plus two equaled five.

Lillian Alter Park was a good-looking woman with coarse gray hair "done" with a sophistication beyond what Parnassus could achieve (she went to Pittsburgh once a week just for that purpose) and sensual lips, which seemed to mouth over each word when she talked. She was Rutherford's second wife, and her father had owned the bank where Ruddy worked.

Ruddy had long admired Lillian before their marriage. Even in high school he would say he thought that Lillian Alter was pretty hot stuff. In those days, however, Lillian was considerably above Ruddy on the social scale, and she also had bad family problems. Her branch of the Alters, despite owning the bank and being so rich, was terribly mean with money ("Tight as the paper on the wall," was how Aunt Charlotte put it). Old Mr. Alter was so stingy that the only thing the children had for breakfast was coffee soup, which was hot water poured through grounds of the dinner coffee from the night before. And some of the Alters were downright crazy. Lillian had a brother, Fred, who would go on rampages with the butcher knife and have to be put away in Torrance, the local asylum, for a time.

So all in all, when Ruddy Park had run off years and years ago with a girl named Mary MacIntyre and married her, it was just as well. But over the years he had never stopped thinking and talking about how much he liked Lillian Alter. Finally one day Mary had heard once too often how wonderful Lillian Alter was, and she said to Ruddy, "Well, if I die you can just marry Lillian Alter, and that will be fine, because all the Alters need is one more nut in the family."

And then, when she was in her fifties, Mary Park was diagnosed as having cancer and she did die. And Ruddy, one year to the day after her death, did marry Lillian Alter. And Aunt May, as the town's social and moral arbiter, decided this was not to be condoned. She conspired with Ruddy and Mary's daughter, who was married to an army officer down South, and she let it be known that she did not intend to invite Ruddy and Lillian to her house.

Finally, Lillian Park had to call on May and bring her a Royal Doulton figurine as a peace offering. Then May, graciously accepting the tribute, invited the Parks to Sunday evening supper, although, as she pointed out to my mother, the figurine—it was "The Balloon Woman"—was chipped. Lillian said she had chosen that one because the face was so sweet, but of course, typically of the Alters, she had chosen it because it was on sale.

May's moral authority on the occasion was all the more remarkable, because at the same time she was ostracizing Ruddy and Lillian, Jack Love was calling her at home frequently, as well as spending all day with her at the Keystone Dairy office. He was at the time in the throes of his second or third divorce, and with anyone else one divorce would have been cause for May to cast them out of God's knowledge.

By the time I was partly grown up, after my parents, Chauncey and Lucille, had moved away and I was in school elsewhere, when I would visit in Parnassus for two or three days, May's relationship with Jack Love had stabilized into its final phase. He no longer stopped at the house except briefly, and he was never mentioned except occasionally as "Mr. Love" (in response to which my mother used to mutter, "Remember, May, we have met the man"). But May, now retired from the dairy store and keeping books in the mornings for the Buick agency upstreet, stopped at his house for an hour or two every afternoon and the telephone rang as often and unpredictably as ever.

One June evening when I was there for an overnight visit between the end of the college year and going away to work for the summer, I was sitting on a stool in the corner of the kitchen, where I had a direct line of sight along the hall to the front door. The evening outside was pale green, and the light was as clear as the oval pane of glass in the big front door. I saw the familiar stout figure with the flapping gray gabardine coat and the snap-brim fedora come up the porch steps.

"Aunt May," I said, "there's someone at the door."

She put down the spoon with which she was stirring gravy for my favorite swiss steak and walked with her usual deliberation to the door. I, with the excessive delicacy of youth, turned my back and began to study the blue and white graniteware canister set on the countertop.

After a few minutes she came back into the house (she had stepped out onto the porch); later Aunt Charlotte came back from the church where she had been helping to tally membership lists, and we had dinner and played several rounds of three-handed dummy bridge.

The next morning Aunt May said to me, "What happened when Mr. Love brought the paper last night?"

I said, "Well, he came up on the porch, and I turned to you and said, 'There's someone here with the paper,' and you went out to get it."

"That's what I thought," she said. She paused for a moment, standing beside the dining room table where I was sitting and resting her hand on the lace cloth. On the third finger of her left hand she wore a silver ring fashioned like a clover leaf. "He thought you turned away because you saw that it was he," she said. "He's sensitive about that sort of thing."

I assured her, volubly lying, that I had not known who it was.

She started into the kitchen and then stopped. "Don't you turn against us," she said.

Jack Love's relegation to the front steps, never to be admitted to the hall, let alone the parlor, was almost entirely Charlotte's doing. Scrawny, always moving about, hair gleaned into a knot at the nape of her neck, Charlotte complained (only within the family, of course) that May domineered and bossed her in every detail. She was afraid, she said, to so much as order an extra quart of milk without checking with May (although May was perfectly generous about money). And indeed my mother would chuckle about May reading the ads for new spring dresses in the paper and saying, "Charlotte, any one of these three dresses would look good on you. I'll call Horne's and have them sent out on approval."

But Charlotte, for all of her remarks about "I'm a nervous creature," had ways of exerting her will that may not have changed all that much since she was a girl in charge of the younger May.

In 1951 the Pennsylvania Turnpike was opened as the first toll "superhighway" in the nation. Now, it happened that one of the accesses to the highway was near Parnassus and another near the Pittsburgh suburb thirty-five miles away where my parents and I had moved by that time. Using the turnpike changed more than an hour's tedious trip through downtown Pittsburgh traffic into a half-hour breeze. The pleasant last part of the old way, rolling up a tree-lined boulevard along the Allegheny River and then over Cockscomb Hill to drop down into Parnassus as though it were Oz, was cut off, granted, by using the turnpike, but the gain in efficiency and good tempers more than made up for the loss of the picturesque.

Charlotte, however, heels dug into the nineteenth century, not only would never fly in a plane in her life, she also did not much like cars and she loathed the turnpike. So with every command invitation to Sunday supper issued by May (something of a sore point with my mother in any case), there came a rider issued by Charlotte that we were not to use the turnpike. "Charlotte's afraid you'll be killed," May would kindly point out.

Finally, one rather tense Christmas, May, feeling the gap perhaps more than usual between what might have been and what *was* in her own life, had been particularly insistent in her quiet way on our paying frequent visits to Parnassus, and when she relayed the message about the turnpike, my father responded with

"Hell's patoot, I'll drive the damn car on the railroad tracks if I want to."

May had issued her invitation one Sunday afternoon for the following Sunday. Apparently she hung up, told Charlotte what my father had said, and retired to her chamber to recover her composure. An hour later, when she came downstairs, the living room was completely dark except for a pool of yellow light under the iron bridge lamp in the far corner by the glass-fronted bookcase. Charlotte, a crumpled shadow in her dark winter dress, sat in the armchair beneath the lamp, crying.

"What's the matter with you?" snapped May.

"I'm afraid they'll have an accident on the turnpike and they'll all be killed. Boo-hoo-hoo," wept Charlotte bitterly, crumpling her handkerchief to her face.

"Oh damn it to hell," said May, using her very strongest oath, as she turned to the telephone. When she called our house she got my mother, who said, "I'll give your message to your brother—he's very angry and he is a grown-up." (My father was fifty-five years old at the time.) My father swore again, and my mother said to him, "Well, they're old ladies and they were very good to you—they sacrificed a great deal to put you through college—so we could do it this once and then just not say anything about it again."

That was perhaps the prototypical winter evening that I remember so well of driving over Cockscomb Hill in the cold gray dusk with Parnassus lying down below, not only promising warmth and comfort, but also twinkling with the lights of power from whence came The Law.

The turnpike anecdote was used by May to justify her side of things when people's faces lengthened as they heard her snap at Charlotte or heard Charlotte say, "I'll have to ask my sister whether we need any fresh strawberries" to a vendor at the door, or reply to an invitation to play bridge, "I'll have to ask May. . . ."

Charlotte and May's relationship was established in the past, of course, but it was a past that had begun before their own lives and one that May tried to hand on—specifically to me on one grim Presbyterian Sunday afternoon in an act that would resonate through my life.

I was about six years old, and that Sunday must have been ordinary in its ritual. In memory it is a kaleidoscope of events from all Sabbaths.

In church the interminable sermon eventually ended, the minister inveighing against Catholics and sin. Then there was an infinite moment of total silence when the whole sanctuary and congregation hung suspended in a bubble between heaven and earth, between the murmur of prayer and the mutter of gossip, after the last drawn-out quaver of the old choir's seven-fold amen.

"The Lord watch between me and thee, while we are absent one from another. . . ." The old warning, given by Abraham to Lot over a border dispute, so appropriate to the heirs of the wrangling Scotch-Irish who sat beneath the minister, was repeated in church as a benediction. The rustling of hymnbooks and coats swelled to a roar of talk.

Sometimes I ran off to the choir room, where Aunt Charlotte and the other ladies who sang in the choir changed out of their robes. I opened the paneled door to a chorus of elderly virginal shrieks. The ladies had taken off their plum-colored robes and stood, not revealed, in sleek nylon "slips." But though they shrieked, they were not displeased, because when Mr. W. K. Henley, the aluminum company executive, paused in the doorway and said jovially, "Ah, a choir of angels," everybody laughed.

I was startled by the ladies' shrieking, and I wondered—at that age—about the difference between what people said and what they meant. If the ladies cried out at me, why did they laugh at Mr. Henley?

At Aunt May's, when we got there, the table was set. There were the lace tablecloth and the damask napkins. "This is the good Haviland china," my mother would say, tapping a plate with little blue flowers on it with her bright red fingernail.

That china sat at five places at the table: one for my father at the head of the table, one for my mother, one for me, and one each for Aunt May and Aunt Charlotte. Aunt May cooked importantly in the kitchen, an apron over her good church dress, while Aunt Charlotte bustled back and forth, filling the water glasses with ice and putting the relish dish of olives and celery on the table and waiting to be told when she could mash the potatoes. May communicated with her in short, negative barks that electrified Charlotte into spurts of activity. Charlotte talked to herself the whole time with little jerking argumentative shakes of her neat head, raising her eyebrows and shifting her dentures in her mouth. My father, reading the paper in the living room, his suit jacket still on, of course (he would not come to the table without it), his big stomach thrust up by one leg thrown over the arm of the overstuffed chair, turned his head toward the kitchen and chuckled, "Dutch is talking to herself."

Later, as dinner wound down to its well-fed conclusion, Aunt May, complacently folding her damask napkin before she stepped out to the kitchen to dollop the spoonfuls of thick whipped cream onto bright yellow lemon pie, said, "I'm really a country girl."

"But you haven't lived in the country since you were a child," my mother said, knitting her brow petulantly at May's fantasy of being a simple woman. "In the country—" May moved slowly and deliberately down the sloping dining room floor of the old house out to the broad, low kitchen, while Charlotte, clearing the plates, fussed around her progress like a yapping little dog. "In the country there aren't all these false politenesses and people pretending all the time, like they do in town—why, in the country folks were natural."

On the particular Sunday I was to remember for so long, the afternoon stretched on enfolded in its warm gray cocoon. Inspired by boredom, I asked Aunt May if I could go up to the junk room. "Why surely, if you like," she said in her musical voice, and she and I proceeded up the steep, narrow stairs. In that old house on Fifth Avenue, there were four bedrooms. After my father got married, May and Charlotte each kept a bedroom, one was kept as a guest room in case an elderly cousin came in from the country for a few days, and the fourth had gradually gotten filled with cast-off furniture and memorabilia from other parts of the house.

At the top of the stairs there was a low platform from which one more step on three sides led to the other doors and the back hall to the bathroom. I was always cautioned to be careful there because one false step could send you plunging back down the staircase. Aunt May opened the door to the junk room on the right, and I stepped carefully up into a block of cold, damp air, sealed off as the room had been from the earthy, soft-coal warmth of the rest of the house.

I reached up to the light switch. Three naked bulbs stuck into an ornate porcelain fixture in the ceiling shed a glare over the room, which seemed dimmed by the foggy cold. The room was cluttered with a spinning wheel, trunks, and rather threatening piles covered with sheets. On the striped wallpaper there hung a large picture in a dirty gilt frame of a frowning little boy wearing a sailor hat on the back of his head and standing beside a very peculiar-looking plant. "That," said Aunt May, coming up soft-footed and heavy behind me, "is our brother Chalmers, who died of diphtheria when he was only six years old—your age. He died before your father was born."

I remember having trouble believing that he was Daddy's brother, if he had never known my father, and Aunt May explained in her patient and superior way that things that belonged to the family in the past were still part of the family today. The spinning wheel she said had been given to my great-great-grandmother by a woman named Massy Harbison who was captured by the Indians in the long-ago Revolutionary War days. "Almost all of her children were scalped," said Aunt May, "and she only escaped because the Indians fell asleep around their campfire and a flock of robins sent by God showed her how to get back to the Allegheny River—that old river that's right down here at the foot of Bridge Street. Some white men were going past in a canoe"—I visualized them cruising past in the way our neighbors drove past our house in their Dodge—"and they rescued her."

Aunt May paused and then said solemnly, "She was very brave."

She moved over to a hump-backed old Saratoga trunk. "Look!" She opened the trunk. "Mama's sidesaddle used to be in there, but I guess it got too rotten to keep and we threw it away." She poked at some of the things in the trays across the top of the trunk's space, and then she lifted them out. Below there were folds of rusty black cloth. "That," said Aunt May, "was my mother's good Sunday dress." She took it out and shook it, holding it up by the huge puffed sleeves with its high-boned collar sagging between them. The dress was black, faded to an iridescence as many-colored as a butterfly's wing. I was transfixed by it. The power of the past hung before me.

"You can try it on," said Aunt May.

I was muffled and smothered in mothballs and dust, then, with the folds spreading around me like a sorcerer's cloak, I was exhilarated. I pranced and leaped around the junk room.

On other visits my favorite object had been a high old mahogany Victrola. Now I went over, pushed up the lid, opened the doors below, and selected one of the brittle records. After vigorously twirling the handle and listening to the record begin its slow moan, I laughed at the reedy plaint of Harry Lauder singing "Keep the Home Fires Burning."

"There's the hat." Aunt May squashed a round black circle of crushed feathers onto my head. Massy Harbison's Indian captor's crown transmogrified by gentility.

"I want to go downstairs," I said.

"Be careful now, don't trip. Hold it up," said Aunt May.

I stepped haughtily down the stairs into the front hall and through the door of the living room.

In the room there was a startled, "Oh now look what he's got himself into," from Aunt Charlotte followed by her barking laugh. Aunt May said, "Isn't that cunning?" And my father, looking startled, said, "Where did that come from?"

But my mother's face, I remember, hung horrified as a mask of tragedy in the Sabbath gloom.

*   *   *

Twenty years later when Aunt Charlotte died at the age of
eighty-five after a heart attack at a bridge club (where she liked
being better than anyplace in the world except choir practice), I
was a young man living in New York, and I had begun to wonder
about relationships—those of all degrees and denominations
from which I felt so closed off.

Charlotte died in June. Most Parnassus funerals seemed to
take place in the spring or summer, as though the old people
there conserved their strength through the winter (and consider-
ately left their families with winter memories of warm lamplight
and good dinners rather than of dank graveyards), and then
when spring came the frail hearts seemed to feel that the need for
perseverance was past and, surprised, simply stopped.

Aunt Charlotte's funeral was a last grand Parnassus occasion.
My parents picked me up at the airport and nostalgically drove
me along the sluggish Allegheny, over Cockscomb, and down
into Parnassus, where Aunt May's house, I knew, would be fully
stocked with cousins and Jell-O molds of all flavors.

The maples lining Fifth Avenue met over the street, darkening the brick pavement and making a tunnel out of which I
stepped from the car into the glare of the slate sidewalk. The
shabby, huge old houses sat back, a little hesitantly, on their
pocket-handkerchief lawns. Behind the screen door I could see
dim figures moving in the front hall, and I had the sense that
had scared me when I was a small boy of reserves of people moving about in back bedrooms and pantries. There always seemed
to be quick, light steps and creaking boards, drawers shutting,
and breaths of sachet after everyone was supposed to be ac-
counted for.

Aunt May met me at the door. We looked at each other
dumbly, unhappily, and I noticed that her black eyebrows, posed
like quotation marks, which had contrasted with the white hair
for so long had begun to turn white themselves. She and Charlotte had not been people for gestures of affection so we did not
touch, although my mother flew between us and hugged her.

Jack Love had died about five years before, after calling May at six o'clock in the morning to tell her that he had terrible chest pains. She counseled him to lie down on the floor, which had often helped such pains in the past, and when she called back at eight o'clock there was no answer. The town fluctuated between ignoring the death—as they had been taught to ignore his life—and treating May as something of a morganatic widow. My stepgrandmother, Ruby, who was someone who understood people's needs, drove May out to the cemetery to visit Jack Love's grave once.

And now May was bereft of Charlotte—"independent," as she had so often said she wanted to be.

At the funeral home—a Fifth Avenue mansion converted for the purpose by one of two rival undertaker brothers named Proudfit—all of old Parnassus came to pay their respects that afternoon and into the long June evening. Ruddy and Lillian Park came, and Lillian confided to my mother, mouthing her words as she always had, that "Charlotte was my friend. When May didn't want Rutherford to marry me, Charlotte went to him on the sly and told him that it was just all right." A country-woman in a clean, faded gingham dress who clearly hadn't had any teeth for years stood in the line next to Lillian Park in her summer silks. When the woman's turn to speak to May came, she said, "You people was always kind to me when I was in high school. You always let me rest on your porch when I had to wait for Pap to come in town to pick me up." Mrs. Oblonsky, the Polish washerwoman, came in with tears streaming down her fat red cheeks, and hugged Aunt May.

That evening I sneaked away from a supper table laden with gifts of ham, fried chicken, and lime Jell-O clouded with carrot strips. I took my father's heavy Chevy station wagon and drove out from under the trees on Fifth Avenue to Second Avenue down by the river where the houses were bleak and cooling in the evening light from a day of shadeless sun.

Colored Hallie lived in an unpainted shack of two stories on the back of a lot. When I knocked at the screen door, she called in a high voice that seemed to be a variation of Aunt May's company voice, "Hellooo . . . I'll be right there." Then, when she saw me, she said, "Oh, honey boy," which was what Aunt Charlotte used to call me.

Hallie hugged me—she was a little, plump, very dark woman with a jagged scar in her throat that had fascinated me as a child. I asked her how she was, and she said, "Well, it's just like Bessie Smith or one of those girls used to sing, 'You was a good ol' wagon but you broke down now, baby.' "

She said yes, she did want to go see Miss Charlotte. "Oh, Miss Charlotte and me had such good times together; she had a real hearty laugh with me, different from what she had with other folks. That morning she died—they took her to the hospital, Miss May said, after her attack at club, and that morning Miss May come in when I was dustin' the chifferobe in Miss Charlotte's room so it be pretty for her when she come back, and Miss May said, 'She's gone, Hallie,' and I just went down plop on m'knees—I just had to go down." Hallie took a handkerchief out of the pocket of her Sunday dress—an old navy blue silk one of Aunt May's—and wiped her eyes.

As we pulled up to the funeral home, she said, "You know, I always say, Miss Charlotte 'n' Miss May, they help me to raise my girl Carrie. My Carrie's six years old when I go to work for them."

This was puzzling because I knew Carrie was not young. "How old is she now, Hallie?"

"She's fifty-eight," said Hallie proudly.

After Hallie had been in to see Aunt Charlotte, whose profile was as crisp as her personality had been among the oleaginous spread of satin shroud and waxy flowers, I drove her home. Thanking me and chattering, she got out of the car ("Now you tell your mama and daddy to come see me"), and with a rush of tenderness I reached for her hand and pressed it. She immediately shot me a look, sharp as a bird's when it sees a worm, and looked down at her hand. I remembered, too late, that whenever my mother stopped to see how Hallie was, she always pressed a five-dollar bill into her hand as she left. Shame made me blush hot as the bygone afternoon sun.

But when she saw that there was nothing there, Hallie became her warm, talky self again and, with a last wave of Aunt May's navy blue sleeve, was gone.

When my parents and I returned with May to her house after the evening visiting hours at the funeral home, it was a hot black night with the trees pressing close against the screens on the open windows, rustling like ghosts. Occasionally there was a cry from one of the few trains that still found its way up along the river line.

In the morning I woke feeling the heat pressing down on me as though I were lying under two woolen blankets instead of just a thin crisp sheet. There were sounds of movements downstairs, of course. I looked at the clock. It was eight-fifteen. When I got downstairs my father was already sitting in his shirtsleeves on the glider on the porch reading the paper. Aunt May, stooped and heavy, was moving around the kitchen. In the living room, which was dim but not cool, I speculatively touched Lillian Park's Balloon Woman, sitting on top of the bookcase in the corner. I explored the rough surface of the chipped green balloon that for twenty years had marked May's power.

By the time my mother came down, the table was formally set for breakfast with grapefruit spoons with serrated edges and the second-best English china.

"Lordy, I feel like I've been parboiled," my mother said, fanning herself with her napkin. "Dear, look," she said to my father. "May's cut the grapefruit so nicely. At home he complains that I just sort of haggle it to pieces, and to tell the truth, I do."

"Looks lovely, but grapefruit's too much work to prepare and too much work to eat," said my father, manfully tackling his portion.

"Well, there's rolled oats, too; I got up in time to put it on to simmer," said Aunt May. "Charlotte always made the oats, but I can do it."

"Oats! On a day like this," said my father.

"Charlotte always liked oats." May started out to the kitchen. "She got up early enough to make it. In fact," she said with a sadness that was more feeling than any tone I had ever heard her use about Charlotte, "she got up much earlier than she needed to in later years."

As she put the steaming bowls of gummy, grayish oatmeal punctuated with little brown points of raisin in front of us, she said, "I like oatmeal."

And then I knew that the reason that May had never become independent was that she had not *wanted* to be. "Move out," my father used to say to her complaints, and of course she never did because she couldn't. She was the brave superstructure—the elaborate Victorian manse with its fanciful gingerbread and proud façade—but Charlotte was the foundation.

Charlotte had won. For eighty years May had laughed at Charlotte's oatmeal, and here without question, on the morning of Charlotte's funeral, we ate the despised oatmeal—not as funeral meats that would have been meet as homage—but as the proper breakfast for all time.

Aunt Charlotte's funeral bore out my revelation of the morning, and so did subsequent events. The funeral was one of the best attended Parnassus had enjoyed in years. The minister characterized Aunt Charlotte as "an institution," and everyone I had ever heard of in family anecdotes appeared onstage, performing perfectly in character. After we came back from the cemetery, when various old friends—the Parks, of course—and the family were sitting on the front porch, an ancient Packard pulled up at a walking pace along the curb.

"It's Mrs. West," whispered my mother in awed tones as a fat old black man got out and opened the back door for an equally fat old lady with a powdered white face and a red wig, worn under a stiff hat with a little cockade of feathers on it. It was indeed Mrs. Emerson Euwer West and her chauffeur Wallace Waugh. Mrs. West was the widow of the owner of the coal mine back in the valley behind Parnassus that had first provided the fuel for the mills three-quarters of a century before. Mrs. West, once the common young wife of the foolishly fond old mine owner, had ascended decades ago on his death to an otherworldly ether filled by Florida mansions, a Pittsburgh apartment (in addition to her big brick house in Parnassus), and High Living. The aunts censured her when her name came up, but they respected her too. She always maintained a liberal pledge to the Parnassus Presbyterian Church, and she was the bridge to the Big World.

Now, asthmatically wheezing at the foot of the porch steps, she surveyed all of us.

"Well, this is really old Parnassus," she said. She held her hand out for a little cream-colored condolence note, which Wallace Waugh passed her and which she gave to Aunt May, who had majestically descended two steps to greet her. When Aunt May introduced me, the only person there under sixty, Mrs. West said, "Now with your Aunt Charlotte gone, you must defer to us, young man. We're the only ones left of the old town residenters."

Aunt May didn't last very long after Aunt Charlotte's death. Her strong mind began to fail, and she took to keeping notes in a little book she carried with her of anecdotes she wished to tell, so as to dominate the conversation still at bridge club and dinner. She retained her serene commanding appearance; once when my mother was meeting her at the bus stop in Pittsburgh because she could no longer find her way to Horne's alone, she got off, said Mother, "looking like a million dollars. She hardly knew whether she was afoot or on horseback, but she was wearing her good navy blue coat with the silver fox collar and a navy blue straw hat, and with her white hair she looked like she owned the street."

May died after she was mugged one dark night late in winter by some teenage boys from down by the river when she lost her way walking home from the grocery store. They blacked her eye and broke her shoulder. After several days in the hospital, she went into a coma and by the time the days were lengthening into spring, she was dead. The doctor told my parents that he didn't know why she had died. "Her injuries weren't so bad," he said. "Of course she had arteriosclerosis, but her heart was strong."

The answer was that where there was no will, there was no way.

And that was the end. . . .

Except for one last doubt that I now have about the neatness of the story. As the minister eulogized May at her funeral, noting her business acumen and her contributions to much of the town's commercial and cultural life, I had felt satisfied that I knew the secret of her strength. It was, I had thought since the morning of the oatmeal, the presence of Charlotte. And surely May's collapse at Charlotte's death proved that. But no road runs only one way. And I remembered now that when Aunt Charlotte was in the hospital in the few days between *her* heart attack and her death the summer before, I had called her from New York. She had been dozing, apparently, and a patient in an adjacent bed answered the phone.

I asked for Miss Kincaid—the formal title, of course, for both Charlotte and May.

The woman called to Aunt Charlotte and then came back on the line to tell me that "Miss Kincaid isn't here, but her sister is."

INTERLUDE

IN Parnassus there were the powerful Kincaid aunts, May and Charlotte, who shaped so much in our family's life, and three great-aunts, my mother's Stewart aunts, as well: Aunt Mabel, crazy and mean, lived alone in an apartment over a store on Ninth Street because none of her sisters could live with her. Aunt Myra, monumental and disheveled, sat among piles of DAR record books and family papers in a house at the top of Monticello Hill. Aunt Hallie—whose name was the reason for Colored Hallie's unthinking racist tag—was sarcastic and grand; she boasted oriental rugs and smoked cigarettes in a large square house down on Sixth Avenue, built by her executive husband, a big man in the bathroom-fixture business in Pittsburgh.

My mother's father, Lucius Quintus Dinsmore, lived in the country, eight miles out the Puckety Creek Road, on the fragment of the Revolutionary War land grant awarded to the fife-playing grandsire. He lived in a bungalow with his second wife, sultry Ruby, now become stout and capable, and his bachelor brother, Roscoe, a withered gnome who drank and was a Democrat. Across the road, in the dilapidated family farmhouse, lived another brother, Vic, and his wife, Carrie. "How are they all in the country?" my father would ask when my mother had run out the creek road in our tan Plymouth coupe for a flying visit.

Town on the river and farm up the hollow.

They were the complementary hemispheres of an America that had been there since the first white settlers crossed the mountains.

May and Charlotte, in their ever-present circling of the lives of my mother, my father, and myself, actually sometimes formed a strengthening web that wove itself around my mother in a way she had relied on from her childhood.

When my mother was thirteen, her mother, Jean Stewart Dinsmore, died of pneumonia. Quint Dinsmore, dapper, the pride and joy of his family, and extravagantly self-indulgent, mourned all on his own behalf. He made Lucille his companion in his sorrow: He became Edward Barrett mooning over Elizabeth before Robert Browning burst in to carry her off; he was every Victorian father with a pretty daughter who was there solely for his own delectation. "I was never allowed to spend a night away from home after my mother died," my mother would say, "because it upset my father too much."

The refuge for Lucille from this attention were the hard, corseted bosoms of her five aunts—Jean's surviving sisters: Mabel, Myra, and Hallie in Parnassus, and Edith and Bertha who lived in the West. All but Mabel were married, but only Hallie had a child, so that Lucille could pick and choose among them and play them off against each other. All were sharp-tongued and imbued with overweening family pride. "My great-great-grandfather was a ship's captain from Northern Ireland who jumped ship in Philadelphia so that he could fight in the Revolutionary War," Aunt Myra, the family archivist, would say. It was only when I was an adult that I realized he was, of course, a common sailor—why would a captain desert the ship in which he had bought a share? Nonetheless, deck swabber or officer, his passport, dated 1774, granted him the privilege "to paff and repaff from Grt. Britain to His Majesty's Dominions on His Majesty's lawful Busineff," and it hung, ancient and awful as the

Ten Commandments, on Aunt Myra's brocaded dining room wallpaper. The Stewart aunts took young Lucille to Pittsburgh to shop for clothes and entertained her teachers for lunch and gave parties for her. They even, defying Quint's prohibition, took her on trips, one of which was cut short when a telegram reached the vacationing merrymakers saying, RETURN LUCILLE HOME SOONEST FATHER VERY ILL.

When Lucille stepped off the train, however, Quint, miraculously recovered, was there to meet her.

And then Lucille went to college and Quint, within a year, married a smoldering and beautiful young teacher, Ruby Boyle, who was only twelve years older than Lucille and, at thirty, fifteen years younger than Quint. Lucille, feeling cast out, nonetheless worked to get along with her stepmother who, in a more emotional way, worked at getting along with her. For ten years they lived together while Lucille taught school.

My mother was a pretty woman in the 1920s style when the ideal for feminine good looks was just that: pretty rather than beautiful. Gertrude Lawrence, Billie Burke were in her line. Her mouth was a perfect Cupid's bow, and her eyes were green; her face was oval and she used those green eyes to great effect, casting them up like a silent screen actress, the dewy lips just parted over the pearly teeth. She adored any man she was talking to. Oh, you great big strong man! Was it love at first sight or was it a joke? Being alone with her was a party. She was friendly and devious, and you never, never knew what she was thinking.

When she married handsome Chauncey Kincaid, his old-maid sisters, living a block away, were the kind of relations she was used to. She became their dear little girl, just as she had been for her own aunts.

Chauncey Kincaid was the handsomest man alive. "People on the street used to stop and turn around just to look at your father," my mother would say. But despite his good looks and ease of manner, he too was scarred by his difficult childhood. With his mother dying when he was so young, only eight, and his father leaving them so that May and Charlotte had to keep up appearances and pay the rent, he came to indulge in a lifelong melancholy. As indolent as he was handsome, he learned early on that people would do things for him if he just presented himself. As he used to say, he became a teacher because he was sitting on the front porch glider at the right time. His sisters had said they couldn't afford to send him back to college for a third year when Mr. W. G. Dugan, a plump, fussy man who was county superintendent of schools and had the aura of a small-town potentate, despite a considerable stutter, walked by. "Ch-ch-chauncey," he inquired, "wh-what are you going to do this f-f-fall?"

"I don't know, Mr. Dugan."

"Well, I've g-g-got a sch-school out in the country you could h-have."

And so, for the next forty years, Chauncey was a godlike pedagogue who felt he had wasted his life.

When Chauncey and Lucille married after going out for a blue moon, they were both still children in their hearts. Steeled in the changes of a capricious world, they had each learned that their fetching ways and good looks would please the choir of ancestors behind them.

And then, after many years of marriage, they had me. And that made three of us: Chauncey, Lucille, and me—all children in comparison with the old folks. Three children, chafing under and outwitting, but oh so depending on, the old people.

We were who we were because they were there. And they had been there, and their fathers and mothers before them, forever.

THE FARM

I

1822

In the Name of God Amen. I Conrad Ludwick of Franklin Township Do make, constitute and ordain this my last Will and Testament in the name and form following: . . . I will and bequeath to my beloved wife Mary over and above other bequests hereafter mentioned the sole use and possession of the new house, situate over the run from the Old Mansion House and also the privilege of using the Spring, Springhouse and the cellar during her natural life, also I bequeath to my beloved wife Mary the one third part of the live stock, all her wearing apparel, bed and bedding, a table, her saddle and all the kitchen furniture. . . .

1950

IN the mornings, before I was old enough to go to school, my grandfather, Quint Dinsmore, would come for me in his red Studebaker and we would go for a ride. My grandfather would say:

What's my name?
Pudd'n 'n' Tane.
Where do I live?
Down the lane.
Ask me again and I'll tell you the same.

I thought the lane must be like the lane at the Farm, where my grandfather lived. What we called "the Farm" or "the country" was a piece of land with an old farmhouse and its buildings on one side of the road and a cottage, built by my grandfather and stepgrandmother Ruby in the 1930s, on the other side.

The lane wound up through a hollow across the road from the cottage to the white farmhouse sitting under its great old brown barn up on the hill. That was the only real lane I knew, and *lane* seemed to be a mysterious term to me; it seemed to be the way of getting somewhere that would be magical when you arrived. I knew of no other streets or roads or highways or sidewalks that could also be called lanes. And the farmhouse itself at the end of the lane was the most important thing I knew of all the *things* that filled grown-up lives and meant more than they seemed to. The Farm was the source of all plenty and comfort, and people's passions—I felt then but couldn't know—swirled around it. My grandfather made hurt, jealous remarks about Vic, his brother, and Vic's wife, Carrie, and what they were doing to the farmhouse itself where they lived, and my father was always angry—in a curt way—when my mother let me go to my grandparents' for supper or to stay overnight. He was jealous, I think, of the idyll they offered me at the Farm where they would say, "Now what would you like to do?" and the choices, although predictable, were infinite as far as my freedom to choose. My father always said, "He gets sick every time he goes out there, because they feed him too much."

My father also shared the sense of abundance the Farm offered, however, because, after I had been there, he would say, "How are they all in the country?" and the rich sound of his voice when he said "the country" suggested that he took pleasure in all that I knew to be there. His voice as he sat back in his heavy platform rocker with the mahogany swans' heads on the arms and his big belly thrust forward called up hamloaf and home-cured bacon and peach pie and Lady Baltimore cake and seven sweets and seven sours on the table and strawberries hidden under the copper-green leaves of the strawberry patch and overheated coal fires and overstuffed chairs and the white, misty smoke of strong cigars. So the Farm was a resource and a source of jealousy and comfort, and the farmhouse at the end of the lane was the center of the Farm.

Getting to the Farm meant my grandmother riding in with my grandfather to pick me up. "Now we're going to have a big time," Grandma Ruby would say. We then drove the eight miles out of town. There were, on the way, hints of stories and signposts, some indicating the stories that would come at the Farm, some not, but I never knew what would be picked up and turn out to have significance later.

We first drove out of Parnassus along the flat road that twisted beside Puckety Creek, through West's Hollow, the mining town owned by Mrs. Emerson Euwer West, where a long white building of row houses was set into the hill. It was nicknamed The Titanic, "because it looked like a ship," Grandma explained without clarifying anything for me. The road was cut between sections of hill that began to swell up as we moved away from the river. Here and there were pieces of another road, looped around the hill above like scattered bits of a broken necklace. Grandma said, "There's the old road—the way we used to go. They really paved the cowpath when they built that one." Sections of the old road ended sometimes in crumbling asphalt hanging over a cut in the hill. Grandpa said, "When I was a boy and we came to town in the horse and wagon, we had to ford the creek five times. The horses' fetlocks would get wet and freeze and they'd clatter like sleighbells."

When we got to a crossroads eight miles from town, we were almost at the Farm. We paused at the stop sign. (My father said on our way to the Farm, "I own this corner." "What do you mean?" I asked, and he said he had drifted through the stop sign once and a cop, sitting silently in his patrol car behind some bushes, drove out and gave him a ticket, but I did not know why this should mean he owned the corner.)

My grandfather usually said, "All this land belonged to the old people."

Across from the stop sign, there was a green shingle tavern named Denny's sitting bleakly in the lap of the hills where the roads met. Its isolation was fitting. It was a bad place. They served liquor there and I knew, for that reason, nice people shunned it. At night an orange neon sign glowed malignly out across the road; inside I imagined it must be murky and illumined by flickering points of light. Denny's was not a place that stories were told about; only dark occasional references were made. And yet, Uncle Roscoe from the Farm went there. He backed his high old Plymouth out of the garage every night after supper and was gone. No one said where, no one spoke about his not being there, and when I asked Ruby she said, "He's gone down to 'the corner' " and shrugged her heavy shoulders.

(*In the Gazette of August 16, 1809, Ebenezer Denny, as Chairman of the Pittsburgh Moral Society, pointed out that, although vice was probably no more common in Pittsburgh than in other youthful towns, nevertheless much might be done to combat it by ministers and magistrates and by keepers of taverns and ferries. He made an especial appeal to parents and guardians to secure more strict observation of the Sabbath.*)

Opposite Denny's, set up high above the road, looking down on it, an old, old stone house, the color of crumbling mud, offered a counterpoint to Denny's and presaged the antiquity at the Farm. In fact, this was the original mansion house of the first ancestor who set up his sawmill and trading post. But that I came to know much later. When I was six years old I just knew that at the Farm there was the smell and feel of something older even than the endless tales everyone told.

The mystery of objects—and the stories attached to them like tattered wrappings—pervaded contact with my grandparents. The "things" were manifold and ranged from two-hundred-year-old broken farm implements to what Grandpa called "the latest wrinkle." They loved gadgets out at the Farm (much, I would later know, as Benjamin Franklin and Henry Ford and Thomas Edison and all those anonymous Americans whose models crowd the archives of the Patent Office loved gadgets), and they had, among the antiques crowding the little rooms of the cottage, crystal sets and cabinet radios and clock radios and plastic letter racks jumbled together. In the kitchen Ruby had one of the first electric carving knives ever marketed, and she had a whole historical set of General Electric mixers, each superseded by a newer model as it came out; there were egg poachers in that kitchen and doughnut makers and pressure cookers and pie pans with little metal strips fastened to their centers, like the hands of a clock, that you could move around under the pie to keep it from sticking. All of them suggested lives of such order that there was an occasion and a proper time for every small event. Cooking was not defrosting and heating something to be slipped out of an aluminum receptacle onto a plate; it was a deliberate process with both the preparation and the result serving as complimentary halves of the same ritual, and each variation of the ritual requiring its own implements.

When I was a child, the only form of egg that I would ingest, finding the other kinds too raw—"slimy," I thought—were hard-boiled ones. My mother either sliced the egg in unequal slices with a paring knife or gave it to me to eat whole, and I was careful to bite a large portion of the end away because I could only stomach the white if I also got a mouthful of yolk. But at the Farm—an example of the precise anticipation of every need—they had (the most wonderful gadget in the kitchen) a simple wire frame in the shape of half an egg that was jointed in two halves that could be brought together across a hard-boiled egg and would cut it cleanly into six slices.

1830

*Inventory of the goods of Abraham Bolanger Deceased
this 12th Day of April 1830 Franklin Township*

Family Bible Germon . $8.00	Lot of Books 1.00
6 Pewter Plates 2.00	Lot of Pewter Dishes 6.00
6 do spoons 25	1 Bed bolster & Beding 3.00
Bee hive & Lot 3.25	Cask of flaxsees 0.50
1 Cask. 1.25	Spinning Wheel 1.75
Bed beding & Bedstead . 5.00	1 Ditto. 2.00
1 pot 1 Kettle & Skillet . 1.50	Coper tools 3.75
Lot of augers & goug. . . 1.12¹/₂	Rake Tools 0.87¹/₂
2 hammers & pincher . . 1.12¹/₂	Lot of chisels and compas saw . 0.75
Saw square & Sundrys . 1.50	Stityards heckle & shell 3.50
Sifter. 0.50	arm Chair. 2.00
4 chairs 0.50	Lot of farming utensils 3.75
1 axe. 1.25	Table. 1.00
	56.00

Many of the Farm gadgets were ancient and sat rusting in fields and gathering dust in odd corners of outbuildings and garages. They seemed to tumble down out of the hollow where the farmhouse and springhouse sat—the springhouse covered with unpainted boards so old that their whorled surface was bristly—past fields where cultivators rusted and the barn where leather harnesses rotted, to Grandpa's house where fragile berry boxes, bins of tools, and a tin tub with a washboard lying in it rested in the attic above the garage, wrapped in dust. From the corroded copper apple-butter kettles hanging on cranes in the maw of the springhouse summer-kitchen fireplace to the battered aluminum saucepans discarded in my grandfather's basement— where there was always a rotten-egg sulphur smell from the septic tank—there seemed to be movement toward the modern in these fossils, like the layers of ancient villages that were destroyed and rebuilt and destroyed and rebuilt until the archaeologist can slice through them as neatly as Ruby sliced through a four-layer cake at a church bazaar.

One morning on my ride, my grandfather said to my mother, who had come with us, "Well, we have a new gadget out at the Farm."

"What is it?" I asked.

"Oh it's a surprise. I can't tell."

I thought of things for me—tricycles and pogo sticks—but decided it wasn't near Christmas or my birthday. "Guess," my grandfather directed. I could never stand the suspense of guessing, and my mind went blank. "It's something you look at," he said. Then I knew. "A television!" I was awestruck.

Driving back from the Farm at night, after my parents had come to pick me up, you could tell who had television and who didn't. In that great black space that was night and that frightened me with only lights winking on the dashboard of the car at my eye level and sudden pale washes from a streetlight breaking the dark, some houses would have an eerie blue light shining out from otherwise dark windows. The shimmering light seemed to dissolve the frames of the window it shone through. "They have television," my mother would say, in the tentative tone one uses about people who have been converted to a religion you don't understand. People in those days turned out their lights to watch television at home the way they would have sat in a dark theater to watch a movie. And no domestic tasks were undertaken, which was different from the way women had sewed and men read the paper while listening to the radio. Instead, the families who had television lined up their chairs, night after night, and solemnly watched I Remember Mama and Dragnet, the blue light shining out across the lawns.

It was right that at the Farm, where every gadget had a story, they would be the first in the family to own the ultimate gadget—one that told stories itself. The night I first saw the television confirmed my father's idea that the Farm was a bad influence on me because I threw up when I got home and was too excited to sleep. But it wasn't the television itself, nor just the excitement of self-indulgence and too much stuffed flank steak and corn pudding that made me sick; rather, the television stirred the same deep pools of imagination that stories about the things at the Farm touched.

For the most part, however, the associations with the discarded, arcane gadgets interested me even more, with their only suspected uses, than any modern one could—even television. Ruby and all the great-aunts, because they were schoolteachers, instructed me a lot, though they did not necessarily explain things (such as why Uncle Roscoe went to the corner). For instance, I had been told by one of them about Benjamin Franklin inventing bifocals. All of the important people I knew—which meant all of the adults—wore glasses and I was intrigued especially by the notion of Benjamin Franklin's spectacles. One evening when I was at the Farm for dinner, talking about spectacles, my grandfather said abruptly, "There's some spectacles up at the farmhouse, I think. If they're still around, you can have them. We'll go up and see after supper."

He muttered something to Ruby, who shrugged the dismissive way she shrugged when I asked about Uncle Roscoe and turned back to the dishes she was drying.

It was October and just sunset; five o'clock supper was finished. My grandfather came back from the hall closet putting on his gray felt fedora and holding out my jacket for me. I struggled into it, hurrying after him as he selected a stick from the umbrella stand by the sun-parlor door, but Grandma called me back with, "Here, Pudd'n 'n' Tane, let me fasten your jacket. It's getting cold out there." I stood in one place, though not without small jerking movements of my arms and shoulders, until she said, "Stand still" and then jerked the zipper harder than I had been twisting. Then she said, "All right, don't cross the road without Grandpa," and I followed my grandfather's slender form as he stepped in a deliberate, elegant way across the yard. You had to climb down a little path through a honeysuckle terrace onto one side of the highway, "the berm" as my grandfather called it. This was dangerous because big cars and trailer trucks the size of buildings, it seemed to me, thundered past. That night, the air was as bracing as a wet, cold cloth on a hot forehead, and the grass, anticipating frost, seemed to crunch slightly underfoot. The road, when we got down into it, was dark, although the sun still brought out the gold and red of the trees on top of the hills, like colors in a paisley shawl. There was a scary patch of walking along the berm, after we crossed the road. I hugged the hillside but Grandpa, courageously, walked on the edge of the road to keep his feet from getting muddy and tapped his stick on the pavement. Then we were at the foot of the lane that led between the hills up to the farmhouse. It was paved in chunky red-dog, the brownish refuse from the mines, and it climbed gently through the little valley—Grandpa called it a "holla"—beside a brook—which he called a "run"—to the house.

"This run used to empty into the dam and millrace down at the old sawmill that stood down by the creek," he told me. "When I was a boy, you could still see the wheel, though they didn't use it anymore. Vic just let it fall down, like everything else—just sat there and let the Farm fall apart and be sold out from under him." He shook his head in his "oh my" gesture, and then recollected that he was talking to a child and said no more.

We approached the house, which was L-shaped and covered with vertical white clapboards. It sat to the left of the lane with an apple tree, crooked and splayed against its side like a sort of natural trellis, and on the other side of the lane, backed up against the hill and approached by a little bridge over a creek, the two-story springhouse leaned.

The farmhouse was the oldest thing I ever knew—even later when, as an adult, I saw buildings in Europe that were centuries older they never gave out the feel and smell of the past in the same way, with wood worn to the texture of earth and layers and layers of paint and grease rubbed smooth as wax applied again and again. The back portion of the farmhouse was a log cabin that had been covered with clapboards when the front portion was built in the 1860s. By the back door, where the underside of the porch roof joined the wall, the clapboards did not perfectly meet, and you could see two rows of logs. They were chinked with yellow mud and wasps made nests of paler mud there. The white clapboards covering the rough logs were like Grandpa's stories of his boyhood at the Farm that sheathed his resentment of having lost the Farm, of how things were now. Where the stories did not quite meet there were glimpses of older times, as humble and primitive as the logs.

When Grandpa pushed open the plank door into the kitchen that evening, the smell of damp wood and stale canned stew and coal pushed against the cool earth smell from outdoors. The kitchen was dark and low, with the wallpaper above the gas stove as thick with grease as a butter dish left out on the kitchen table too long.

Carrie was there. She turned and said to my grandfather querulously and with no cordiality, "Come in, come in," making sharp little movements with her hand.

Carrie was bent and small with frizzy gray hair standing up all over her head and horn-rimmed glasses. She had been the housekeeper for a cousin who was a neighbor, and Vic had courted her in a laconic fashion for twenty years. Then when Vic's aunts died, Carrie said he had to marry her. He was sixty and she was fifty. When I was a child, he was in his eighties and Carrie had control of the farmhouse. They said she was cunning; she had warts.

"Vic's in the front room," Carrie said. We went through little square rooms to the front of the house where Grandpa's brother, Vic, sat in front of a coal fire. The coal soughed and exhaled, settling in the grate, glowing more deeply orange. Vic was small and dry; he leaned crooked in his chair and seemed lost in his billowy white shirt. He had a long, lean face marked with vertical lines like the clapboards of the house and a shock of gray-white hair. Supposedly he had hardening of the arteries—or maybe he had had a stroke, no one knew which—and so his voice, nasal and stuttering, curled thickly around his words as though there were more in his mouth than his tongue.

Actually, there was more in his mouth than his tongue because he chronically chewed tobacco. When my grandfather, at home, would deplore how Vic had "failed," as they called it, saying rather fussily, "You can't get more than one word out of three that he says," Ruby would reply with a snort, "Yes, he's failed all right; he's failed to chew his plug of Mail Pouch as good as he used to."

My mother always said that Vic had started to chew tobacco because, when he was a young man and living in town before he came out to take over the Farm, he had been a paperhanger and housepainter and the smell of the paint made him sick. Chewing tobacco was supposed to counteract that. But Ruby would turn to my mother and say, "They always claimed that, but it was just an excuse to chew, if you ask me."

And my mother, who tried to preserve faith in what was told her, would look wounded.

The evening I visited the Farm with my grandfather, Vic nodded once or twice and said, "How're ye?" Grandpa, without responding directly, answered, "He"—often in the family they called me "The Boy" or just used the masculine pronoun; I was the only son, the only child, the only grandchild—"wants some old spectacles. There's a box of them here someplace. Back under the stairs, I think."

There was a pause while Grandpa confronted Vic collapsed in his chair and Carrie hovered behind me. "I wouldn't know," she said. Then tension stretched between Grandpa and Carrie across Vic until Carrie, unable to prolong it even for her advantage, pushed Vic's shoulder and urged, "Quint says there's a box of spectacles here. Is there?" Vic nodded and began to pull at the arms of his chair and shift his cane around so that it was exactly angled between his feet and sure to trip him. "Here, here," Carrie pushed at his shoulder to help him up. "You'd better come git it yourself." It was partly because of the way Carrie talked that Ruby called her "shanty Irish," and it was because she was shanty Irish that the family so resented her having "the say" over everything at the Farm. "Oh, Carrie's the power behind the throne up there," Ruby would say. So tonight Carrie pushed at Vic to hobble and get the spectacles himself.

She could, I now know, have just said they weren't there, or that somebody else had taken them. Vic would never have opposed her. But she could afford to be magnanimous. My grandfather was testing his right to assert two hundred years of ancestry over Carrie's circumstantial present power, and it worked—but only because Carrie chose to let it.

It was supposedly Carrie's presumption of Vic's good manners that had brought about their marriage. "Vic and Carrie were just a case of proximity, that's all," my mother and Ruby would say and nod sagely to each other. "He was much too good for her," they would continue, wiping the red-and-white dishes with castles on them, punctuating the familiar rhythm of the phrases with dishes that Ruby lifted from the soapy basin to the rinsing basin of her sink (those two basins another example of the mechanical elegance at the Farm), and Mother wiped with a circular movement, letting them elide from her hands to the stack resting on the counter. "Vic was a gentleman. That was his trouble. He wouldn't have had to marry her, but he was too much of a gentleman not to."

We stood in the middle room of the farmhouse, stooped Vic and Carrie and my grandfather, erect but frail (still holding his hat either because Carrie had not taken it or because he did not mean to sit down and capitulate himself to her hospitality). Gray light came from an iron lamp with a paper shade by the window, and when Carrie dragged open the door of the cupboard under the stairs, it was a blacker hole in the dim room. Vic pushed and gestured with his cane until my grandfather impatiently bent and pulled a cigar box from under a gunny sack. "Here." He handed it to me. It was a Flor de Gusto cigar box; the lid had gaudy colors picking out the name and a picture of a palm tree. I opened it and there, wedged together like the pieces of an intricate puzzle, lay cases of cracked leather and silk and tin. I gave a cry of delight and promptly sat on the floor (still wearing my outside jacket; my grandfather had not taken it off for the same reason—whatever it was—that he still held his hat). I began to pull through the cases, opening them and discovering gilt pince nez—"nose glasses"—on thin chains, round tortoiseshell frames, and then, in lozenge-shaped tin cases, tiny square or oval spectacles. Some were split in the middle of the lenses—like Benjamin Franklin's first bifocals—and some of those had adjustable sections in their bowed earpieces that slid to greater or lesser lengths. "These were just what I wanted," I crowed, and Grandpa said, "Good, he can have them, can't he?" to Carrie, who answered, somewhat irrelevantly, "I thought some was here."

"Whose were they?" I asked.

"Oh, Aunt Mattie's and Aunt Mary's."

"Those nose pinchers were Aunt Mattie's," said Grandpa. "I mind when she got them; she said they were too good to feed the chickens in and she went back to her old spectacles and only wore these to church." He chuckled and then, warming to the subject, bent over and poked around in the box himself.

He pulled one case apart from the other with the finger he wore his Masonic ring on. "These were Grandpap's, I think." He took out a tiny oval pair. "He wore these when he read the Bible at night. He slept right in this room," Grandpa said. "The bed was there." He pointed to the corner by the window. "The winter I was fifteen I spent out here, and I slept with him—that was 1895; Grandmother was dead. At night we went to bed about eight-thirty, nine o'clock. He'd read his Bible by the fire and then he'd blow out the lamp and put on his nightshirt and get in; there'd be a rustling, it was a corn-husk mattress, you know, and then he'd commence to snore. I'd lie a while longer by the fire and read for school—I attended Sardis Academy. There was an old copybook here someplace—it was Grandpap's—it had his name in it, and his dad's before him. It went back to the seventeen hundreds, I think. . . ." But Carrie made no further move to find things. Grandpa went on, "After 'bit the fire would start to die down and it'd get so dark and cold that I couldn't read any longer but I couldn't bring myself to stop. Well, finally, when I couldn't pick out the words, I'd strip off my clothes and jump into bed wearing my long johns, and Grandpap would say the next morning, 'You woke me up with those cold feet again.' "

My grandfather added solemnly, "They were good to me."

I sat on the floor surrounded by my plunder, and Grandpa said, "Come on, now, we'd best get back down the lane." He must have said thank you to Vic and Carrie; I don't remember that I did. I just remember that when the kitchen door opened we walked into a void of dank night air. The door slapped shut behind us and as my eyes got used to the dark, the night seemed blue-silver with stars pricking the sky above the darker mass of the hills. I sang a song to myself about the wonderfulness of spectacles, and Grandpa, who liked to tease, said, "Now you can see the way they saw."

He said to himself in his proud, hurt voice, "There's a lot of nice things up at that farmhouse. It's a great pity what's happening to them." But he seemed almost as much to enjoy watching the decay of the farmhouse, and its placement securely in the past, as he would have the actual struggle of living there.

On Saturday mornings Vic and Carrie would deliver eggs in their Model A Ford to the families in town who had supported the proud barren Farm for years. As a very small child I was frightened of them and the car. The noise it made was, Mother always said, "like a thrashing machine." I had never heard a threshing machine but I thought the noise was like one of the last trains that came into Parnassus, which I was taken down to see and which—as it swelled massively along the track toward the station, with steam hissing from the wheels as the brakes were applied—seemed to fill all the space around me with its clanking, crashing, pumping roar so that I was inside the sound completely, tossed and tumbled by it.

When Vic and Carrie's car arrived at our house one morning, my mother suggested that I ride with them as they delivered their eggs around town. I was frightened, but I knew I had to go. I got into the car with the certainty of being devoured. How interesting it was, instead, to have the innards of the whale (I, the small Jonah, sat on the gear box between Vic and Carrie in their cracked leather seats) turn out to be sticks and dials and a big stiff old wooden steering wheel that Vic turned by pushing it up

from the bottom, rather than by turning it overhand, as my father turned his steering wheel. Carrie's brown oxfords—just below my eye level—were cracked like Colored Hallie's but they
seemed appropriately old rather than inadequate as in Hallie's
case, and her stockings were cotton lisle, opaque, beige, with
little nodes of thread sticking on them.

The eggs, which they sold for 60¢ a dozen to the McSparrens,
the Parks, Mrs. West, Aunt Charlotte and Aunt May, could only
have brought them in five or ten dollars a week. Chicken feed
bought at Hamilton and Alter's Feed Store, located across from
the town hall and set in the middle of the mills, run by a distant
cousin of Great-Aunt Myra's who only "made a go of it" because
his father had found coal under the family farm, was $3.00 for
a twenty-five-pound sack, and the gasoline for the Model A on
its trip into town was 25¢ a gallon. So it took three or four stops
with eggs even to pay for the trip—and then the profit was a dol-
lar or two.

That was how things were at the Farm when Quint, my grandfather, took me up for the box of spectacles. By then the two
horses were gone, the pigs and cows had been sold. They kept
chickens and Carrie made a garden. Otherwise there was no income except from the gradual sale of the land: ten acres here, five
acres there.

Finally there would be left only the land around the house
and springhouse and a few feet on either side of the creek beside
the lane.

A few weeks after I got the spectacles, Grandpa took me on a
long walk up to the top of the lane above the farmhouse and
back through the autumn woods to the few stones piled against
one another that was all that remained of the log house where
he was born. He showed me the foundations of his birthplace,
and then he picked up several blunt-ended rusty nails that lay
among the stones and he gave them to me as a memento of the
day. They were like sacred relics from a shrine—a shrine that was
both the ruined seat of a dead religion and at the same time an
active shrine to the past.

The spectacles and nails were the first of a flood of objects. The next visit Quint gave me a pen made of glass with a blue shaft and a clear, sworled point that he had seen an itinerant glassblower make on Ninth Street in Parnassus when he was a boy.

As the years went on, more and more came to me from the Farm. I was immersed, submerged, inundated in things, things, things—and then there were the papers. Among the first that I saw was an English copy of the German will, made in 1822, of Conrad Ludwick, my great-great-great-great-grandfather, who had been a Pennsylvania German fifer in the Revolution. From those papers I came to know this about Conrad and his farm and how it came down to Vic and Carrie:

The Allegheny Mountains are among the oldest on the planet and therefore they have been worn down, smoothed off, until they are rounded and ridged, not sharply majestic like the Rockies. They were domestic in scale, one thought, driving along the cramped curves of the Pennsylvania Turnpike when it was new in the 1950s. Going through the dark tunnels built in the 1830s for the Pennsylvania Canal, which the turnpike designers appropriated (tunnels that Aunt May would never traverse; she couldn't breathe in them, she said), you felt that these mountains were manageable; they are known through their social, human history. These are not the Alps where Hannibal and Napoleon became mere historic shadows in the face of eternity.

Nonetheless, in the late eighteenth century and until the opening of the Pennsylvania Canal, these mountains constituted the most daunting natural obstacle to settling the American continent that Europeans had yet encountered. Between Carlisle at the foot of the mountains in the east and Bedford in the west, there were seven major ridges, some more than 2,000 feet high, and the trip from Philadelphia to Pittsburgh took at least three weeks on a surefooted horse. The distance was 350 miles. There were panthers in the woods in those days and bears, and it was only couriers, of course, who had the privilege of a surefooted horse. Most people—that is, settlers—walked with all their earthly goods, quilts, plowshares, grain, and the wheel for a spinning wheel (the one part of that essential appliance that a farmer could not make for himself) strapped onto a packhorse or two. Then the trip was very long indeed.

When the travelers had attained the foothill region around Pittsburgh they were glad to settle in the fertile creek bottoms and try as best they could to cultivate the steep slopes of the smooth-topped little hills that pushed tight against each other with only narrow valleys between.

My Stewart grandmother, Quint's first wife who died long before I was born, used to say about the farmhouse, nestled deep in its hollow, that you could look up the chimney and see the cows coming home.

My great-great-great-great-grandfather, the Pennsylvania German fifer, had bought the farmland by cashing in the depreciation certificates he was given for piping his way through the war. His pay, in new Continental currency, wasn't worth a Continental damn in the postwar inflation. So they gave him land.

The early German families had lots of children and lots of food—they were the only frontier folk who ate salad greens. German cabins were the best built and the most comfortable inside with puncheon floors scrubbed white, covered with rag rugs, and sometimes, as a great luxury, a wavery-looking glass hung beside the door, wreathed by colored birds' eggs and red peppers and topped by sprigs of evergreen, like a household idol. But the German settlers lived a month's journey from their church schools in the East among hellfire-minded Scotch Irish. Horseshoes were nailed over doorways to keep the Devil out. At Christmastime a fearsome figure called the Belznickel man went from farm to farm dressed in a coonskin cap, a mask, and a pantherskin cloak with a tail dragging behind; the mask might be the snout of the panther with the Belznickel's eyes glinting through the eye holes. Bellowing and capering about, he frightened the children and then, warning them to hang up their stockings and get to bed early, he promised to come back and fill the stockings.

My strong-willed, frivolous mother, the heir of that Farm's ways and its beliefs, would say with a speculative gleam in her eye, "There's not much that I'm superstitious about, but I don't like a bird flying against the window, trying to get in. That means somebody is going to die."

No one had made a living from the Farm for decades; my grandparents drove into town every day where Grandpa sat in state in his real estate office holding half the deed boxes in the county, and Ruby, bosom thrust forward like a flying buttress, was principal of the elementary school.

Wraiths of beliefs—and of humanity—hung about that Farm like cobwebs in an attic. My mother was the heir in spirit to the Farm, but the last family member to really live there was Carrie, whom I thought, as a child, was a witch.

The day I knew that Carrie was a witch was when I was about six years old and my parents had brought some friends out to the Farm. I was a pampered only son, while these people had a little red-haired girl who was skinny and had asthma and mosquito bites the size of red strawberries all over her and her little brother, who was four with a huge head covered in blond hair and mournful blue eyes. This child seemed to trust his conniving sister, contrary to all the evidence in his life.

The girl had just persuaded us—against express prohibition— to cross the road, along which the trucks rampaged, to the field that belonged to the Farm proper. Great-Uncle Vic leased it to a neighbor who had planted it in corn. Now this was August and the corn was high. The rustling shocks cut into our bare arms and legs in our sunsuits and shorts, and the rows stretched confusingly before us, the tops of the corn two feet above our heads and the vista down the row obscured by the mote-filled shifting haze of sunlight and corn dust, white-hot and choking as steam.

The visiting girl, a fiend from hell herself, proceeded to torment me and her little brother by running off and hiding in an adjacent row of corn and then jumping out at us if we tried to find her, or sneaking up on us and calling one of our names in an eerie voice from another row if we stood still. She had just proposed that we play hide-and-go-seek and separate—which made little Dickie cry big silent tears, welling from his baby blues and gluing his eyelashes together—when there was a rustling in the next row of corn. All of us, including bossy Melissa, froze. Then we saw Carrie making her way between the cornstalks in the next row. She was no more than three feet away; any one of us could have reached out and touched her, but she was rather deaf and didn't know we were there. She was stooped, making her way along the row peering intently ahead, with her frizzy hair, warty face, and spectacles in profile to us. She was holding a gray rough feedsack in one hand and every so often the other brown, sinewy hand would shoot out and twist an ear of corn off the stalk and drop it in her sack. An ear of Mr. Ridenour's corn. An ear of corn to which she had no right.

I was digesting this frightening realization when Melissa hissed in my ear, "It's a witch!"

"Ssssh . . ."

And then, so silent were we all, including Carrie stepping softly in the dust, that a sparrow pecking at an ear where the husk had split open didn't hear Carrie, and we saw, quick as an adder's tongue, her hand dart out and grasp the bird. A crescendo of cheepings mingled with the rustling of the cornstalks, then Carrie dropped her gunny sack and with her free hand quickly twisted the little thing's neck.

We were frozen for another few infinite seconds and then we ran, little Dickie holding my hand like his fingers were a tightened noose, with his other hand caught up by Melissa in some atavistic sisterly reaction. We ran, gasping for breath in a pure ecstasy of terror, linked together in a crazy dance that nearly became a dance of death when we burst out of the cornfield, plunged down the honeysuckle bank, and were almost sucked by the vacuum of one thundering ten-ton tractor trailer into the path of another.

The only real casualties were little Dickie's powder blue

shorts, which he had thoroughly wetted, and my peace of mind, which was destroyed for months by the image, coming before me as soon as the lights were out at night, of Carrie's hand holding the bird. Needless to say, it was impossible to tell anyone what I was scared about.

These were the particulars of Vic and Carrie's marriage as they had come down in family folklore: Vic had been trapped into marrying Carrie because he was a gentleman. He courted her down at the end of the lane where she lived for twenty years. He took her for dinner every Sunday into town, where his widowed mother lived with widowed Quint and young Lucille, and he took her to the movies on Christmas and the Fourth of July. When Aunt Mary and Aunt Mattie, the old-maid aunts at the farm, died in the 1930s, Vic must have felt panic at being left alone with his feeble-minded sister, Effie, whom the aunts had brought up and who would giggle and then throw tantrums, breaking crockery and kicking furniture like an animal—baffled—in a pen for no purpose. The dreary days ahead would only be torn jagged by Effie's shrieks. Roscoe, another bachelor brother of Vic's and my grandfather's, agreed to come out from town with an old-maid sister and live at the Farm, but they wouldn't come until electricity and a telephone had been installed. One fall Wednesday, with the hills going scarlet and gold, a load of telegraph poles appeared on a high-cabbed Ford truck trying to negotiate the turn from the road down into the lane. Carrie, picking late chrysanthemums—russet, frosty yellow—in the garden her aunt let her make at the corner of the lane in her spare minutes, Carrie, bending and picking off dead leaves, wearing her apron made from a feed sack and her gingham housedress, saw the truck with the poles make the turn.

Perhaps, as she realized what the truck meant, her shoulders sagged. Then, with a tearing as audible to her as the ripping of a dress caught on a nail in the barn, she heard her heart pull apart. All those years, all those years emptying her aunt's slop jars and cooking and scrubbing plank floors and enduring her aunt's ill temper, all those years had been redeemed by Vic. He took her to town. She had a beau. When she had first come to her aunt's, a chum, a girl she went to school with (before she had to quit when she was twelve to go to work), had sent her a postcard, "a postal," as they said then:

Hellow Carrie Well kiddo heres the big news Sam and me are getting married on Saturday can you come. It don't seem far if you could get a ride into the depot Lizzie

Carrie hadn't gone, knew she couldn't go, didn't even ask her aunt. But she put the card in her keepsake drawer and when, years later, she rode to town in Vic's Model A Ford, she would think of the postal and think she had somebody now who would take her to the depot; she had a man like Lizzie did. So when she saw the telegraph poles go by, she went cold all over and knew. She felt panic. Vic wouldn't put in a telephone for her. His brother and sister were coming out from town to claim the Farm. To claim her place.

On Saturday Vic came in town to deliver the eggs he sold and he stopped at his mother's. "It won't work," he said. Carrie said he had to marry her.

As an adult I realized how few and specific my memories of Carrie actually were. I was eight years old when we moved to the Pittsburgh suburb thirty miles away from that river mill town and the Farm, and by no means did we always see Carrie and Vic every time we went to visit Quint and Ruby.

I did remember, though, when Uncle Vic finally succumbed to his various ailments at the age of ninety, walking up the lane with my mother on a May evening before the funeral and meeting Ruby walking down the lane toward us wearing a pale green dress the color of the new leaves on the hills around. She had a white silk gardenia pinned to her capacious bosom.

Quiveringly alive as I was that evening, as only an adolescent can be, the present seemed the only reality to me—the very moment of the May evening itself. For the first time it seemed that the past, as a presence, as something to be dealt with every day as Quint and Ruby, the aunts, even my parents did, was separate from the present, different from being alive in the damp, green, shimmering evening.

And then the past, in the form of an anecdote about Carrie, licked out, quick and sharp as Carrie's hand that had wrenched the bird all those years ago, and tore away my unthinking exuberance.

Ruby, bossy, bosomy, and kind, started in when she met Mother and me to discuss how broken up Carrie was at Vic's death. "She just didn't know what to do, the poor little thing," said Ruby as the ladies' dress shoes crunched in the red-dog slag of the lane.

"Come to the country and ruin your feet," my mother muttered when her heel turned and she stumbled.

"So," said Ruby, "I took her to Wainwright's store—she didn't have a thing to wear that was appropriate—and we got her a navy blue suit with a little jacket. She just seemed so appreciative."

"Well, that was nice," said Mother.

"I don't s'pose she'd had anything like it since the day she was married, and, of course, that was done in such a hole-in-the-corner fashion I'm not sure she did then."

"Where were they married?" I asked, always one to pin down details.

"Oh, at a justice of the peace somewhere over tow'rds Greensburg," said Ruby.

"When was it?"

"It was 1934. I know because Aunt Mattie died in 1933, and they couldn't get married till she died. Vic was fifty-nine and Carrie was forty-eight."

"And then you remember," said my mother, "the first Sunday after they were married, Vic brought her into town to dinner and when he came into Grandmother Dinsmore's house we said, 'Where's Carrie?' and he said, 'She's out in the car. She's afraid to come in.' "

This was time-polished family lore. I leaned against a sagging split-rail fence, drinking in the evening, while my mother and Ruby stood in the lane going through the story, point and counterpoint. With confident boredom I expected the ending I had always heard, which was my mother saying, "And so I went out and brought her in."

And then, instead, I heard Ruby's urgent, rather throaty voice saying, "And so I went out and brought her in."

The voice went through my mind with the flash of an old-fashioned explosion of nitrate powder, taking a photograph inside on a dark night, only the exposure in this case, literally the exposure of what must have been a lie, was a double exposure on a film I had thought developed and yellowed and filed long ago. There was one image, vivid as everything my mother always told, of herself, slim and pretty in her 1930s dress, hurrying down the walk to the Ford (that same Ford that had ingested me and then spat me out the day of the egg deliveries) where Carrie sat. Then there was another image superimposed on it of Ruby's large white face, dark eyes, and dark hair.

Which image recorded the event? I knew somehow that my mother, whom I adored, had lied all those years about an act of spontaneous generosity. When you were with my mother you felt like all the world was brightly colored and exciting and possibly magical. She was, after all, the descendant of that Farm where they had hung birds' eggs around a tiny winking piece of mirror and cast spells, hexes, on the neighbors' cattle and corn. But the question of Who brought Carrie in? was a painful reversal of my communion with nature that spring evening. My mother selected things from her past to enliven the dun-colored present, she "put a flower on it to make it pretty," as she would say, looking at a gray dress or a plate of mashed potatoes and meatloaf, and then she handed that livelier past to you. The past had intruded—again—into an evening when I was particularly aware of the present—my own present. Again, just when I thought I knew where I was, I didn't.

While I stood in the lane watching the colors of the evening fade into darkness, Ruby said, "Well, better get on up to the house. They'll be missing us." She continued to talk about Carrie. "You know, when they came down and said Vic was gone, I went up right away and there she was in the awful dirty old kitchen, and I put my arms around her, and honestly there was nothing there but bones. She's justa little bird of a thing. She makes me s'mad I could spit ink, but she's such a frail little thing you have to feel sorry for her."

"She certainly never had much of a life," said my mother.

"Well," said Ruby, "I'm going to tell her to come down and sleep at the cottage for as long as she likes so she won't be so lonely."

"That's very, very nice of you," said Mother. "I'd go crazy stuck back up here in this hollow, but then of course Carrie has always lived in the country."

So Carrie came down and slept at the cottage every night through the summer and early fall, until the weather turned cold. In fact, for the next three or four years Carrie wended her way down the lane every afternoon about four o'clock unless the snow was too deep for her to walk in and, perched on a rocking chair in the sun parlor of the cottage, chirped out a monologue that had little to do with what anybody else was saying. The days Ruby relented from her oft repeated assertions that "enough was enough" and invited Carrie to stay for supper, she invariably accepted. The days Ruby didn't, Carrie left as Quint and Ruby and bachelor Great-Uncle Roscoe went in to the dinner table. She never asked for anything, but she always brought her flashlight so that if she were still at the cottage after dark she could find her way back up the lane. Once every two weeks a neighbor, who had built a modern house in the woods on the other side of the hill and who thought Carrie was quaint, took her to the grocery store.

Then one evening, it was May again and the world had taken a turn around to feathery pale green again, when my mother came home to our house in Pittsburgh from a visit to the Farm.

"How were they all in the country?" Father asked.

"Well, Grandpa and Grandma and Uncle Roscoe were all

right," said Mother. And then she added, "Carrie was there. She's dying."

"What!" I asked. "Are you sure?"

"Yes," said Mother, taking off her lilac-colored spring raincoat and hanging it in the hall closet. "She is." Mother, with all her desire to make life a bouquet, could face reality with startling directness when there was no getting around it.

"What happened?" I asked.

"I guess she came down as usual at four o'clock and she told them she didn't feel well. They sent for the doctor and they were waiting for him when I left. She was lying on the wicker davenport in the sun parlor."

"Did you speak to her?"

"Oh, I just touched her arm and told her I hoped she would feel better. I don't know whether she knew me or not."

Indeed, an hour later Ruby called and said that Carrie had just died. They were waiting for the men from Proudfit's Funeral Home.

And that was the end of Carrie's story. The next time we went to the Farm, Ruby said she didn't think Carrie had suffered much at the end. "It was very peaceful." Pointing to a faint stain on the freshly cleaned green-and-white striped cushions on the wicker davenport, she said, "She just got fainter and fainter and when she went only a little something came out of her."

Uncle Roscoe, who refused to wear his dentures and drank, said spitefully from his rocking chair, "She just came down here to die."

With Carrie's death the farmhouse and springhouse went out of the family for the first time in two hundred years. Two nieces of Carrie's materialized who sold such antiques as they recognized, and the neighbor with the modern house in the woods who used to take Carrie shopping bought the farmhouse to complete her parcel of land. Because there was no plumbing in it she let it stand empty until, eventually, it was bulldozed. Quint and Ruby did get a trunk of family papers, and from that cache my mother sent me some a number of years later. The package, addressed in my mother's perfect second-grade teacher's handwriting, came to the post office on a drab gray street in Manhattan. It was a dank late autumn afternoon when I went to pick it up. A garbage bag near the post office door had burst open; a derelict pawed through it, tumbling sodden newspapers and orange rinds onto the sidewalk. When, wet through, I had taken the package back to my apartment and sat down, another world, clear, three-dimensional (and distant) as the landscape on an old handheld stereopticon card appeared.

What my mother had sent was a copy of the will dated 1822 of the first Conrad Ludwick (as they came to spell it), the Revolutionary fifer. What I had was a photocopy made in the 1950s so that it was done as a negative. The letters were white on a black background and the whole thing looked like a ghostly piece of lace. My mother, with her typical maddening, charming inconsequence, had packed it in a battered Marsh Wheeling cigar box filled with the old spectacles "to keep it company," as she said in her note.

The will began, with Spencerian flourishes, "In the Name of God Amen," seeming to wrap up a whole life, beginning to end, right there. It then went on to speak about fine real things that nobody experienced anymore, such as "the fruit of ten apple trees in the orchard on the hill," and giving the writer's "beloved wife Mary" the "use of a horse of her own choosing whenever she has occasion to ride." The will was full of other detailed directions about the rights of the beloved Mary and the duties of her children toward her. "I will and bequeath to my beloved wife Mary . . . the sole use and possession of the new house" (that was the old log farmhouse where Vic and Carrie subsisted) "situate over the run from the Old Mansion House" (that was the crumbling stone house down by the crossroads above Denny's Tavern that Grandpa always pointed out as we drove by) "and also the privilege of using the Spring, Springhouse and the cellar during her natural life." She was to get "the fruit of ten apple trees in the orchard on the hill such as she may choose, also my son John is to provide for her every year as much flour and Indian meal as she stands in need of and 200 weight of pork." Like Shakespeare's wife, Mary (who had no rights whatsoever as a woman under the law) was left her bed, her clothes, and all the kitchen furniture—with which, presumably, she was most familiar.

Conrad Ludwick was a miller. The creek—or "run," pictographic country word—which began at the spring by the farmhouse and dimpled the bottom of the hollow to join Puckety Creek was just right for a sawmill and gristmill.

All told, Conrad and his Mary had spawned ten children. On his stone house ("the Old Mansion House situate over the run") the window frames were painted blue. He died a patriarch in the land of milk and honey. One of Mary's prerogatives was "suitable stabling for two milch cows" and among her possessions was a "bee hive and lot." Surrounded by love, she would need no more. The will was full of love and plenty; the struggle and conflicts were past (Mary had once had her arm broken by a Seneca arrow), and the valley of Puckety Creek had become an Arcadia. I could only contrast this care with the scrabbling panic for survival of Carrie's life on that same land.

The will, of course, was the starting place and where it all came back to. I marveled at the odor of love that rose, faint and definite, from the looping, lacelike hand.

The house where Carrie lived and worked for her aunt was at the end of the lane by Conrad Ludwick's gristmill. Carrie's garden from which she was to see the telegraph poles taken up the lane was just at the far end of the bridge, and it was from there that she made her way up the lane to tell Vic he had to marry her. He had wasted her time all those years.

    . . . *It is my will that my son John pay to my beloved wife Mary ten dollars yearly . . . and every year during her natural life, also he is to provide for her sufficiently of firewood hauled to the door of her house, to cut and prepare it for the fire.*
In the Name of God Amen.

Part Two

QUINT AND LUCILLE

QUINT'S STORY

BIG: "He's the big man of the town." Better say: "the chief man," "the leading man," or "the great man" . . . Washington was mentally and spiritually a great man, physically a large man; but we do not ordinarily speak of the Father of his Country as a big man.

> —BETTER SAY: A BOOK OF HELPFUL SUGGESTIONS FOR
> THE CORRECT USE OF ENGLISH WORDS AND PHRASES,
> BELONGING TO LUCIUS QUINTUS DINSMORE

JEALOUS of his dignity, my grandfather had been sensitive to slights from an early age. He used to tell about one of the shocking experiences that molded his childhood: a reprimand he received in church. One Sunday in about 1886 Quint was sitting with his brothers and sisters and parents in Hankey's Church, on top of Sardis Hill by the graveyard where old Conrad Ludwick was buried. In the pew in front sat his grandparents, Jacob and Betsy Ludwick, Betsy stiff in unaccustomed corsets and black bombazine. Aunt Mattie sat at the organ to the right of the pulpit, waiting to crash down on the wheezy keys.

The minister, droning on through a full hour-and-a-half

sermon, paused and, in front of the entire congregation, himself leaning tall and black across the pulpit, fixed his eyes on small Quint. Quint had been sitting at the end of the pew next to the wall where a tall window of clear glass loomed above him. The church, a country church, was too small and too poor to have stained glass. Outside, the summer morning was alluring, but Quint knew better than to look out of the window during the sermon. Nonetheless, he had been beguiling the time through the Gospel reading and the sermon that began with "Firstly" and had to go to "Tenthly" before there would be a break for the cold dinner waiting in the wagon. Quint's distraction took the form of twisting the cord of the window blind into knots and braids around his fingers. Now suddenly, in the deathly hush of the preacher's pause, there came the words, "Young man, take your hands off that winda cord and listen to the Word of the Lord your God."

Quint thought, for one soul-searing moment, that it was in fact the Lord who had spoken. It was only the minister, but when the entire congregation with rustlings and cracking noises had turned to look at the small boy, scarlet-faced above his Eton collar, Quint felt singled out publicly for humiliation, as though he had been stood on a scaffold.

That experience stuck with him all his life, and as an old man he would tell it and end, shaking his head, "That was a terrible thing to do to a child."

Quint's sensitivity had been nurtured from the time he was a little boy when he would come down from his parents' house, away back up in the woods at the top of the lane, to his grandparents in the farmhouse. His grandparents spoiled him. He would spend the summer afternoon perhaps jumping out of the hayloft into the haymow or balancing on the edge of the old millrace, and then go into the cool, dark farmhouse for supper.

His grandmother, Betsy, a squat old woman with red hair scraped back into a knot, would walk him to the top of the lane when dusk was filling the hollow to the brim like black German coffee filling a cup. At the rail fence at the top of the hill she gave him two doughnuts—"fried cakes"—to keep him company on the last mile home through the woods. He ran to get home while the sky still showed silver and pink above the trees, like silver foil through the paper lace of an old-fashioned valentine. Once, when an owl hooted unexpectedly at him, he ran so fast that he tore a toenail off on a tree root and never noticed the pain until he got home and found his foot all covered with blood.

When his parents moved to town in the 1890s so that his father could get work in the mills, Quint stayed with his grandparents and Aunt Mattie and Aunt Mary at the Farm. They sent him over the hill to Sardis Academy, so that he could have such education as the backwoods afforded. He grew up slight, though not as frail as his brother Vic, and handsome (in old photographs) with large blue eyes and curly black hair.

He was the recipient of talent and taste in his generation, and he was desperate to improve himself.

He started work as a clerk in various stores around town. Instilled with the idea from the country that they had been people of consequence, the idea come down from the days when Conrad Ludwick had been known as "King of the Pucketoes," Quint found it harder to keep up the notion in the booming mill town. New frame houses defined more muddy tracks as streets every month and his big family jostled for room in their house that was one of an identical row on Sixth Avenue. Quint went to night school to learn the double-entry system of bookkeeping. He worked at McQuaide's Hardware Store on Main Street, where Aunt Charlotte also toiled and where he was promoted to bookkeeper when he finished his course. For entertainment he went to church and one evening he went to hear Christy's Minstrels in the new town opera house. Times were changing.

He liked nice things and he wanted to live well. There was a certain popular gold-plated pocket watch, an Ingersoll, that was offered as a prize when customers had collected coupons given with certain purchases. Now, Quint decided he should have a gold watch, so he just didn't bother turning over the coupons to customers but saved them for himself. When he had enough, he sent in for the gold watch. The company salesman, walking into that store on Main Street with its dusty board floor, walking into the shade out of the yellow brick street, hot despite the summer-lush maple trees, the salesman was irate when he found out that an employee had cheated the customers of their premiums. "Mr. McQuaide stood up for me, though," my grandfather said, "and I was allowed to keep the watch."

Perhaps he felt that he had earned a glittering gilt prize. He had studied for self-improvement relentlessly. After he died, I found two slender books that belonged to him in a crate at the Farm. One was titled *Better Say*. A cloth-covered blue book, it carried the subtitle *A Book of Helpful Suggestions for the Correct Use of English Words and Phrases*. The book described grammatical amenities that seem oversubtle today but that in the first decade of the twentieth century were the mark of a gentleman. It told when to use "shall" (customarily with the first person singular and plural, for emphasis otherwise) and "will" (customarily with the second and third persons, for emphasis with the first person) and gave forthright advice:

> The true French pronunciation of employee cannot be indicated by English phonetics and can scarcely be attained by an English tongue. Better plain, downright English than barbarized French. Compare ENVELOPE.

The other book is called *Mission Furniture: How To Make It Part I*. It was published in 1909. The introduction says:

> This book is one of a series of handbooks on industrial subjects being published by the Popular Mechanics Co. Like the magazine, these books are "written so you can understand it," and are intended to furnish information on mechanical subjects at a price within the reach of all.

By 1909 Quint found it useful to know how to build his own furniture. In 1906, on October 22, his birthday, he had married

Jean Stewart, one of the pretty, sharp-tongued Stewart sisters who lived in a big gray house on Fifth Avenue with their parents. John Alexander Stewart had not wanted his daughter to marry Quint, perhaps because the Stewarts thought the Dinsmores were "beneath them." So Quint and Jean eloped. The Stewart girls called Quint "Ikey" because of his pretty, curly black hair. After the elopement one of the Stewart girls heard a fracas in the house and asked another sister what was wrong. "Jean's run off with Ikey and Papa's mad," the sister answered.

In late 1907 my mother Lucille was born to Jean and Quint. They lived in a house at the corner of Fifth Avenue and Fourth Street, set up on a terrace above a mossy old stone wall. They owned a set of Haviland china, white with little pink roses rambling all over it, and for pleasure Quint sang at weddings and funerals with Isabelle Alter, Charlotte Kincaid, and T. C. Porter in a group called the Mel-o-dee Quartet. He made a tall case clock in the Mission style with upright oak palings framing the pendulum, and he made a small golden oak table for Lucille to sit at with her dolls and their dishes and have tea.

In May, 1913, *The Pittsburgh Sun* noted in the chatty way of newspapers in those days:

Washington, May 29. The President sent some nominations to the Senate today. They included the following:

To be Commissioner of Indian Affairs—Cato Sells of Texas.

To be Solicitor of the Department of Justice for the Department of Labor—John B. Davis of Montana.

To be Postmaster—Pennsylvania—Lucius Quintus Dinsmore, Parnassus . . .

There Quint was, mentioned by the President with the Commissioner of Indian Affairs and the Solicitor of the Department of Justice. He sat at his rolltop desk behind the wire cage in the post office on Main Street and corresponded with the government. He was a man of substance, as he had always thought he should be. He wore pongee suits in the summer and a derby hat in the winter, and he wore stickpins of opal or topaz.

His best friend was J. Moulton Euwer, known as "Moult," who was the youngest man on the Session, the governing board of the Parnassus Presbyterian Church. Quint was not yet a member of the Session but he soon would be.

And then Quint's life seems to have flowed into the mainstream of Parnassus life, the voices multiply, and the pictures called up by the voices are as multitudinous and varied as the quickly moving scenes of a magic lantern show flickering across a sheet hung up in the back parlor for a children's party.

In March of 1921 Harding was inaugurated president and Quint lost his job. A Republican was appointed postmaster of Parnassus under the time-honored system of patronage. And in April Jean Stewart Dinsmore died of degenerative heart failure.

Before that there was another death my mother had known intimately, devastatingly. Before she saw her mother die when she was thirteen, her little sister had been killed when Lucille was six and the little sister was three.

She was hit by a train.

I knew very little about the child and about exactly what had happened. On the wall of the hall outside Quint and Ruby's bedroom in their cottage at the Farm, there hung an oval framed picture of a plump-faced child with golden ringlets à la Mary Pickford. The child looked demurely and rather smugly down at her lap. When I was quite small I asked, "Who is that?" and my grandfather said, in tones of surprise that I didn't know, "Why, that's Louise."

"Who is Louise?" I asked, and Ruby, stepping heavily to the rescue as she always did when my grandfather was in any danger of embarrassment or awkwardness, said, "That was your mother's little sister who died."

I knew, even though I was very young, that Mother was not Ruby's child. (I had been carefully told that while being admonished at the same time to love "Grandma" who had been "very, very good to me.") No danger. I did love her. But it seemed as though Louise, very visible beyond the kitchen doorway but nonetheless relegated to the back hall unlike other family portraits, which hung above the spinet, shared something of the same status as Ruby. So I said, "Was she your little girl?" And Ruby answered in a commendably calm, sad voice, "No, dear, her mother was your mother's mother."

(Ruby's diary: *I have been hurt so often, I didn't think I could ever be hurt again. Lucille always reminds him about Jean.*)

Then, self-control and discretion having been stretched as far as was humanly possible, Grandma said, "She was killed by a train."

And that was it. For years and years. Unlike the details that attached to chronicles of less important events, Louise's dramatic death floated in a mist of silence. Instead of hanging in the back hall, she might as well have been hanging in a dark closet.

Once, I remember my mother saying to Ruby, on one of those evenings when they were doing the dishes, eliding the plates through the dish towels, "I did feel it, though, because my mother said that for two weeks I wouldn't play with my dolls."

"When?" I called from the sun parlor.

There was unaccustomed silence in the kitchen.

"When wouldn't you play with your dolls?" I persisted.

"When Louise died," said Mother. And although I dug and pried, I got no more out of her than that. "You do feel bad when somebody dies," she simply said.

Occasionally Mother would say proudly, "They always said that they could dress me up when we were going someplace and I would sit on my chair and not get a wrinkle, but Louise couldn't be dressed until the last minute, otherwise she'd be out making mud pies in her best clothes." She would pause in these remarks and say, "I always liked to look pretty."

Although I never knew just what had happened, I had the feeling that this black hole in the winking, glittering galaxy of anecdote, reminiscence, and boastful tales of glory that made up the rest of the family history was very, very important. It had affected not only Lucille, I came to think, but also the way her mother and father regarded her afterwards, so that she would feel she could never count on anybody's love and affection unconditionally again.

Many years after the first mention of Louise, when I was grown and helping to clear out Quint and Ruby's house after their deaths, I found a yellowed clipping from *The Parnassus Gazette* of May 1, 1913.

CHILD KILLED BY TRAIN

There was a disaster at the Parnassus Station Friday night when little Louise Dinsmore, aged three, daughter of Mr. & Mrs. Lucius Quintus Dinsmore, of Fifth Avenue, Parnassus, was hit and killed by the 6:10 southbound train to Pittsburgh.

Apparently the child broke away from her parents and was running to meet her grandfather, Mr. John Alexander Stewart, also of Parnassus, who was getting off the northbound train. The child ran away from her grandfather suddenly who tried to catch her, but she was hit by the oncoming southbound train.

The sad part of it was that relatives from the West, Miss Bertha Stewart and Mrs. John Naly, were expected to arrive later that evening for an extended visit.

Again, that was all: the black, heavy newsprint with its old-fashioned smudged edges on the yellow paper, not much more durable than a soap bubble. The image of the child in the white dress (it would be a white dress, company coming and all) blown like a puff of steam from the rushing, grinding wheels of the train to lie on the bricks of the platform. Perhaps.

I said to my mother another time when I was grown and she was old, "What happened when Louise died?"

"Well," she said, her voice on the telephone like a little girl's, "Aunt Bertha and Aunt Edith were coming from Iowa, so my mother had gotten me all dressed up and put me out on the porch swing while she got Louise ready, because you couldn't leave Louise dressed up, she wouldn't stay still for a minute. While I was sitting there a bird flew into the window and stunned itself. (There was a big window in the front living room that looked out onto the porch with stained glass across the top.) I never liked that when a bird flies into a window. Anyway, I don't remember too much else about it"—her voice broke a little bit—"I was only five and a half. Louise was running toward Grandfather Stewart, they said, and she ran away from him all of a sudden, and the 'down train' caught her and just her little shoe was crushed but her head was hit by the step the engineer steps up into the cab on. I don't remember—they went to Wainwright's to get her a new pair of shoes—"

There was silence on the other end of the phone.

Then, "I wouldn't play with my dolls for weeks." Then with her chin in the air, I was sure, as she sat in her room at the nursing home, she said, "And whenever after that I went with my mother to Pittsburgh on the train all of the conductors took off their hats when they saw us."

There were no feelings evident in the rare family mentions of Louise, except the feelings to be avoided. Quint, writing to me at my request when I was in college about the good old days, stated baldly, "In 1913 my daughter Louise was killed. I will not say any more about that as it is too painful."

My mother said once, "When Louise died my mother was expecting a baby and she lost it and it would have been a little boy." So the stern, slender Jean with her bad heart and her clipped Stewart wit was so wrenched by the child's death that she lost another child—and a boy! Oh, the pride for Quint, the farm boy turned gentleman, in that. He would have had a son. Supported and buoyed up all his life by women, it was still the status symbol of a son he would have valued. So highly of himself and his name did he think that poor Louise was named Louise Quintus Dinsmore so that she had the same initials as he. But to have a son with those initials! "Ah, smack," as he used to say when something tasted just right.

But still these are only suppositions drawn from the tiny pile of facts and woven into the most gossamer of attributions. The only feelings that I could actually see and infer belonged to my mother, Lucille, and they were shown in consequences that I came to understand slowly, slowly over the years.

The way Louise's death affected her at first I think went something like this:

After Louise died, Lucille felt completely alone. Louise was not there and Lucille felt terribly guilty because she had begrudged Louise her place in life. Was it her fault that Louise was dead? And then, her mother and father were not there in any way that did Lucille any good. It was as though they and Louise had been taken up together in a cloud of grief and left Lucille behind.

Lucille's father hugged her and hugged her and said, "You're all we have, Lucille, you're all we have. You're very dear to us now. You must make up for Louise not being here." But Lucille didn't know how to do that. And she was afraid that if she didn't make up for Louise they wouldn't love her.

For a long time after Louise died and while her mother was sick in bed, Lucille did not play with any of her dolls—not the two beautiful lady dolls with their hats and vacant faces, not the little china Kewpie dolls with their sideways mischievous expressions (not those particularly, because they looked so much like Louise), not even Raggedy Ann—but then one day she did a terrible thing. She threw the little china Kewpie dolls down on the slate sidewalk, where they smashed to pieces, and then she hugged Raggedy Ann and said, over and over, "We love you, we love you the *best*. You're the one we *always* loved."

When Lucille's mother was first out of bed, just for a few hours a day, Lucille was so pleased. Her mother sat on the porch swing wearing her gown (as they called a robe) and a lacy shawl. Lucille sat beside her on the swing. "Now you belong all to me," she told her mother, who frowned a little the way you do when somebody accidentally touches a bruise.

That afternoon Aunt Hallie came over, bringing her little baby, Jane. Jane cried a lot that day. Suddenly Lucille was furious. "That is a bad, bad little girl," screamed Lucille, her face an ugly red. Then she began to cry before anybody could say anything and threw herself into her mother's lap. "Well!" said Aunt Hallie, but Jean's long, pale face, which could be very stern, looked sadly down at Lucille and she said, "Hush, hush now, I'm here."

"This has been hard on everybody," she told Aunt Hallie. "I think we're a little l-o-n-e-l-y."

I once was telling the story about Louise being killed to some friends, and I said, "My mother is one of the most competitive people I have ever known—particularly with other women—but I don't know why. It seems to me that she won, you could say, by surviving her sister."

One of the friends, a lanky, stylish man who looked like Don Quixote in Italian designer clothes, said, "But she had to be competitive to survive that perfect ghost."

INTERLUDE

WHEN I was a boy I became quite a connoisseur of funerals. I went to my first at the age of seven, when my Great-Aunt Nannie, Quint and Roscoe's squat, old-maid sister, died. Ruby was quite graphic about her death: "Well, she sat down in the rocking chair in the sun parlor and she started to get sick to her stomach, and I got that cleaned up and got her into the bedroom and she lay down and just went into that coma like they do."

Here she was interrupted by my Stewart great-aunt Mabel, who had come to the funeral home in defiance of her sisters who did not like Ruby, and who said, "When Mama died she was like that, and I just shrieked and brought her out of it and *it wasn't the thing to do.*"

What was the thing to do?

"She lived for another three days in great pain," concluded Aunt Mabel complacently, taking full credit for that distinction.

At Aunt Nannie's funeral, my inaugural one, I remember being excruciatingly embarrassed because when I bent my head for a prayer, I fell asleep, and Ruby had to nudge me and say, "Honey . . ." I also remember the crowds and the flowers and the long black hearse leading the procession of cars out to Hankey's Cemetery on the hilltop. It was, I knew, an *occasion* to live up to, for which I as a novice felt woefully inadequate. I didn't realize that participation itself was quite sufficient; feelings were entirely beside the point.

Then, later, there was Uncle Vic's country funeral, held in the farmhouse in that old-fashioned way, where I watched an old-maid cousin of my mother's with bright red hair twist a gold charm bracelet into the skin of her wrinkled wrist during the service until it made marks as deep as scars. After the service my mother, looking at the cousin, said to Ruby, "Madge must dye her hair; she's five years older than I am."

And then there were the funerals of the Stewart great-aunts, ill-attended as they were (they had been recluses for so long). At one of those, Aunt Hallie, who was the youngest Stewart, stood in a corner with a fat woman wearing a polka-dot dress and grinned maliciously as the woman told her about someone named Lillie Lord, once Aunt Hallie's husband's pretty secretary, who was now crippled and in a wheelchair.

There were other, older, darker funerals I knew about where the body itself assumed an importance as great as the occasion. My grandfather once, talking at dinner during a snowy Christmas, gleefully reminisced about a funeral postponed during his childhood because of a blizzard. "Her name was Mrs. McLaughlin," he said, using a guttural to pronounce the "gh" that I found out later in a graduate-school linguistics course had once been common in Celtic-tinged English but had dropped out of use at least a hundred years before. "When it stopped snowing and they came to close the coffin to take her out on a sleigh, they found she'd swollen up s'much they couldn't get the lid down. She was a big woman."

"And she got bigger," my father chuckled.

"Why Quint Dinsmore, whatever do you mean telling a story like that at the dinner table?" said Ruby mildly, putting down stemmed crystal dishes of sherbet to clear our palates.

And there was a little brown scrap of paper, dark and age-foxed as an old person's skin, which Great-Aunt Myra showed me among the Stewart family papers. *Rec'd of the Widow Stewart,* it said, *four pounds for the coffin March 4, 1794.*

"That is the receipt for your great-great-great-great-grandfather's coffin," said Aunt Myra, placing a nail with chipped polish, the color of cinnabar, on the paper. "He was scalped in the last Indian raid in western Pennsylvania, and he was scalped by white men! Renegades!"

But none of these funerals, witnessed or told of, touched me with that dreamlike searching that characterizes the ceremony for someone you love, until Aunt Charlotte's funeral when I was a young man. So, when my mother talked about her mother's death, it was only facts, markers on a hillside like the old gravestones indicating that something of a life lay below.

My mother said once, "You can tell that a dead person isn't really there when you touch their body. It's just like touching cold mud."

"How do you know?" I asked.

"When my mother died, Aunt Myra made me kiss her before they closed the coffin lid. But it was all right. She wasn't really there."

QUINT AND LUCILLE

SMOTHERED by the hagiography that had grown up about my grandmother, Jean, I said once to Ruby I wished I knew something negative about Jean to make her human. "Well," said Ruby, considering, "this isn't really bad, but I'll tell you that when I taught Lucille in school before her mother died, her hair was always skinned back into braids so tight her eyes looked Chinese. Then she was out of school for a week after her mother died, and when she came back her hair was all curly."

After Jean died, Quint couldn't bear to be separated from Lucille, they said. "You couldn't get a broomstraw between those two," according to my father. "Each thought the other could do no wrong."

"When I was in college," my mother said (one of the teachers' normal schools that dotted the state, red brick Victorian towers sticking up above the trees in little county seats, girls with shingled hair running on long silky legs across campus), "Daddy would come to take me out to dinner and I just know people thought, 'Look, there's some old goat dating a girl young enough to be his daughter.' " She laughed, the way she laughed when one of the neighbor men flirted with her.

Because Quint was an elegant man who outshone the rest of his family—Roscoe who worked in the tin mill, for instance—and was the idol of his short, rotund old-maid sister, Nannie, and his mother, Till, he had things the way he wanted. After Harding was elected and he lost his job as postmaster, even the way he went to work was glamorous. He had taken a job at the Standard Sanitary Company in Pittsburgh, a job his brother-in-law, Lawndis Hamilton, had got for him. He was a city man, going to town on the 7:30 train and coming home on the 5:35. At home everyone conspired to make Quint comfortable, and he wore his love for Lucille, his gay and pretty daughter, like a boutonniere on his smartly cut gray lapel.

Then Lucille went to college. Quint began to take out Ruby Boyle. When Lucille came home for the summer after her first year of college, Quint asked her how she would feel if he were to get married again. Lucille looked at him aghast and cried stormily and suddenly.

"We'll say no more about it," Quint comforted her.

("Wasn't that nice of him?" Mother asked me.)

But in October, when Lucille had been back at school a month, the dean of women, a stern, drab woman with emanci-pated shingled gray hair, called her into her office. Rapidly going over in her mind what she might have done wrong, Lucille pushed her arms into her fall coat with the fox collar (it was too warm a day but it was past Labor Day, and the coat was new) and rushed off to the dean's office. When she got there, the dean said, "Your father wanted me to give you some good news."

"Oh?" said Lucille.

"He sends you his love and he has given me the honor of telling you that *you and he* have the *happiness* of his having been married—to Miss Ruby—uh"—the dean bowed her shingled head to look at the note on her desk—"Boyle, Miss Ruby Boyle."

Lucille said in a small, meek voice, "Oh." And then tears, just one or two at a time, trickled down her cheeks. "Thank you," she told the dean. She got up to leave but she did not cry anymore; the dean got up and gently pushed her back into the yellow oak office chair, handing her a handkerchief. Lucille just sat there with a puzzled look, however, so then the dean said to her, "Now, Lucille, your father is still a young man" (which at forty-six in those days he wasn't) "and it is natural that he should want, uh"—her rather blunt hands played with the orange fountain pen that hung on a black grosgrain ribbon around her neck— "permanent companionship. And you must understand that."

It seemed to Lucille as though she had stepped on a rotten well cover over an old well on a deserted farm and plunged into darkness. The dean's kindness gave her just the dangling end of a rope in the black pit where she was. "What?" she heard the dean saying, then "I beg your pardon?" and realized that she herself had been saying something. Her mind was empty now but she tried to collect her thoughts and said again, in the small way, sounding wounded in a way she would at times in her life when she wanted her listener to know she was wounded, "When? I mean, when was he married?"

"Why, I believe"—the dean looked at the note on the polished oak desktop, almost apricot gold in the autumn sunlight— "the twenty-second of October."

"That is his birthday," Lucille said, again evenly, quietly. "It was the day he married my mother."

Then she said again, louder, "We were everything to each other."

Then she thanked the dean and left, feeling as puzzled as a person who, thinking himself to be in a crowd of friends in a warm, lighted room, suddenly wakens to find himself in a bed alone in the dark.

The dean wondered at the romanticism of Quint Dinsmore's marrying on his birthday. It was flamboyant, not dignified in an older man, and it was a bald assertion of ego (which the dean, who had been educated in the East, pronounced "ay-go"). She remembered Quint Dinsmore when he first brought Lucille to campus. She, animated and pretty, Quint, polished—even the dean felt the effect of his good manners—and devoted to each other, they said. Quint had driven over every Sunday afternoon for the first two months Lucille was in college and taken her out to dinner at the Indiana Inn. Well, men of that type had to be fussed over. If Lucille wasn't there to do it, someone else apparently would be found. She wondered how the girl would do in school that semester.

Years later, when I was unhappy in college, my mother said, "I wasn't homesick my *first* year but I was homesick my *second year*."

PARTIES

(*Quint and Ruby*)

WHEN Quint married Ruby he received a cash present from his fellow employees at the Standard Sanitary offices. The money had been given in an envelope with a sheaf of cards, each with a co-worker's name, and tied with white satin ribbons. After Ruby's death, I found the sole memento of that covert wedding in a Horne's Department Store box in her closet.

It would be a Horne's box.

When my mother and Ruby were young women in the late 1920s and 1930s, there was a lounge on Horne's mezzanine where you could wait for friends. The lounge had a book in which you could leave messages for your chums if you had to leave early or had dashed up to Lingerie for a quick purchase while you were waiting; it was an amenity that seemed to belong to a period of orange minks and nose-tip veils, when girls fresh from college, eager with their first salaries, met "in town" for lunch on Saturday.

Ruby, from the years of her first paycheck, always bought at Horne's because it was the "good" store and she, having come from poor people, valued the chance to buy and be seen at Horne's. "*That,*" she would observe, looking at a piece of furniture in a store window, "looks like Joe Horne's while *that,*" pointing at another piece, "looks like Sears and Roebuck—which is just Sears and Sawbuck, if you ask me." *Good* was one of Ruby's favorite words. "Alligator is good this year," she would say to Mother, and I would wonder, Good for what? Good for value on the marriage market this year, I think was the answer, although that was hardly remembered. But, indeed, appearances counted in Parnassus, and particularly in Ruby's experience of life, from the tenant farm where she had been born to marriage with a dignified executive who was a member of what they always called in obituaries "a pioneer family." The appearance in Ruby's case of alluring eyes and a sulky mouth having worked things for her as they did, it made sense that clothes for her were currency. What was "good" any given year had enabled her to win a place in Parnassus Society, and the "good" clothes had rescued her from a fate as a respectable, bridge-playing old maid into a more than respectable marriage.

The Horne's boxes, cream-colored pasteboard with *Jos. Horne Co.* in light, bright blue on the lid, represented for Ruby the life she had made for herself.

When Quint first married Ruby he built a bungalow on the bluff above Parnassus, and when Lucille graduated from teachers' college she lived there with them. Ruby's living room was furnished with a tea wagon, a two-tiered mahogany trolley for bringing cookies and tea bumpily in from the kitchen on rare occasions; her German silver coffee service sat on it. There were window boxes Quint built outside and hand-painted lampshades on the lamps inside. Cunning little lanterns hung from the eaves beside the front door. "We always had the latest wrinkle," Ruby said.

When Mother told me about those days or Ruby reminisced, sitting up late with me over cookies and milk on a cozy winter visit to the Farm, the whole time seemed to have passed in a blaze of glory with the telephone ringing off its stand in the hall and roadsters pulling up and parties. Quint learned to play golf and Ruby learned to play bridge. Ruby learned things that she would later pontificate on to nobody in particular, such as "A lady may always wear a hat in a public dining room."

"We always had parties back to back," Ruby told me, cutting pink and blue and purple asters from the bed beneath the living room window of the cottage at the Farm. "You see," Mother picked up the tale as she bent to pick up an aster that had fallen aside, "you already have your house cleaned and your flowers, so it's no more trouble to have two parties than one." Ruby said, "Your mother would have a party in the evening and then the next day, while she was teaching, I'd have a bridge luncheon."

"Anyway, it was an awfully nice time. And then there was the flood and Grandpa lost his job. . . ."

"Then what happened?"

"Well, that was the end of the parties for a while."

PARTIES
(*Lucille*)

L UCILLE had her own group of friends who hung around Parnassus together. "The Gang," they called themselves, and they played tennis and went to Pittsburgh to shop and entertained each other at bridge parties, when that came in as the new game. The Gang had two distinct natures. One was bicameral and included a set group of boys whom the girls all dated and exchanged among themselves; the other, the real gang, were just the girls themselves. They were all schoolteachers except for Helen Hemphill, who worked in the office at the aluminum company, and Dotty Detwiler, whose father was a doctor, so she didn't work at all.

By the mid-1930s, the gang really recognized itself as the Gang. Lucille and Naomi Vogel were "the bestest of friends," spending weekend nights at each other's houses and talking every evening on the phone after they came home from teaching.

Naomi, who was very determined, got the lead in several Little Theater plays done in town, but Lucille played the comedienne to great bursts of applause.

There were parties of every description. Once between Christmas and New Year's a different member of the Gang gave a party every night—or they went to Pittsburgh to dinner and a show— until by New Year's Day, eating roast pork and sauerkraut at the

Vogels', with Mr. Vogel snoring off his drinks upstairs ("Common!" said Ruby), they agreed they were all sick of the sight of each other.

One of the regular meetings of the Gang was a bridge club they had organized, which met every other Friday night. (The bridge club that I later remembered in my childhood as an antic, be-rouged dance of the girls grown old.) One particular Friday night the club met at the Vogels'. The girls, in their wool sheaths of dark green and cranberry and navy blue with draped necklines and jabots and coming down nearly to their ankles (skirts had dropped along with incomes since the twenties), tripped down the stairs from Naomi's bedroom where they had left their wraps and touched up their marceled curls, to the two bridge tables set up in the parlor and sitting room. With much twittering and giggles they had settled, begun bits of gossip, nibbled some nuts or a piece of candy from the dishes on the table, dealt with carefully assumed nonchalance, and picked up their hands. There was relative silence for a minute or two while hands were arranged, bids were made, and a round or two were played. Then there was a puzzled pause, and simultaneously both tables laid down their hands. There were two aces of spades at one table, two queens of hearts at the other, and various jacks duplicated. "Well, forevermore," said Lucille. "Pa!" bellowed Naomi. "You stacked the deck!" Old Mr. Vogel, wearing his cardigan sweater and with his pipe sticking out of his mouth, looked around the corner of the dining room door, his face cherry red. "I just thought I'd give each of you girls a fighting chance," he chuckled. " 'Taint funny, McGee," said Naomi sourly.

Because Naomi and Lucille saw each other or talked every day, when Lucille decided one evening about a week later that she wanted some red dye to change a pair of silver evening slippers to crimson, she naturally called Naomi, who agreed to meet her in the lower part of town and walk up to Wainwright's Department Store.

It was a crisp, snowy winter night—just cold enough to keep off the damp, but not so wicked as to be uncomfortable if you were well bundled up. Lucille wore her belted school coat, a beret pulled right over her ears, and her galoshes. She pulled her muffler up over her chin while she climbed down the cement steps from Monticello Heights to the old part of town. At the Vogels' on Sixth Avenue, Naomi came right out and the girls walked upstreet. It was Thursday night so the stores were open and the lights of the plate-glass windows gave a festivity to the excursion. There was a fizzy sense of free will in being out on a school night, ducking in and out of the warmly lighted stores as though they were booths at a summer fair. The dye was quickly bought, a couple of records frivolously listened to at Cooper's Music Store, and Naomi said she would walk Lucille back to the foot of the steps.

On the way she said, " 'Cille, honey, what do you think of Luther Russell?"

"Pill," said Lucille.

"I kind of like him," said Naomi, tracing a circle in the snow with the toe of her galoshes.

Luther Russell was a young schoolteacher who had come to town the year before from someplace up the river. He was tall and lean in build, but with a round face that looked unpleasantly full, as though his skin were too tight for the flesh. He had a red, scrubbed look, wire-rimmed glasses, and black, rather damp-looking hair. Lucille, as was always her way with a new boy in town, had flirted and fluttered her eyelashes at him and run her slim fingers up and down his lapel. Luther had remained impervious.

"Would you go out if he asked you?" said Lucille.

"He has asked me." A little smile played around Naomi's lips and she gave Lucille a challenging look.

"And?"

"I've said yes. Several times. We went to the movies last week—remember the night I said I didn't want to go to the cantata at the Springdale Presbyterian Church?—and he's asked me to go to Pittsburgh this weekend to see a play called *Rain*."

"That play's about a *prostitute*," Lucille spat out. She felt such rage that a mist seemed to be closing in around her vision of Naomi's face and below that she felt a panic as cold and churning as the water beneath the ice covering the Allegheny River. It was always like this, always like this, no sooner did she get to trust somebody, to love somebody, to know that they were there, than they left her. Her mother's death, Quint's marriage to Ruby—anybody she counted on left her. It didn't matter that the new person might turn out to be nice; she always had to woo, to court, to beg, to seduce, and then she was never good enough. They always, always, left her. Alone.

Just then an old Ford jalopy pulled up and a man's voice said, "Want a ride, girls?"

"Sure," said Lucille and started toward the car.

"*Lucille*—" Naomi's voice pursued her. "You don't know them!"

"It's Mr. Ommaney," Lucille called over her shoulder, naming an old English housepainter who kept a dilapidated Ford to carry his drop cloths in.

She flung herself into the front seat and slammed the door. The car took off in a spume of snow.

"Hello there, sweetie," said a deep male voice.

It was not Mr. Ommaney. Pressed close against Lucille in the middle of the front seat was a boy a few years younger than she, wearing a tweed cap, and beyond him, driving, a man a little older wearing a fedora.

"You want to go for a joyride, kid?"

"Oh, I'm just going home," said Lucille in a small voice. Her hands in their kid gloves tightened into fists in her lap. "My father is expecting me."

The car, with nightmare slowness, made the hairpin turn on the road.

"You come along with us, we'll have some good times." The boy in the cap turned to grin at Lucille and his exhaled breath rode out on a flame of whiskey.

"No, really, thanks, but my father's waiting for me." Lucille saw the Havemyer house on its bluff slip past the left windows.

She wanted to scream. Argonne Drive, where they lived, was coming up on the right. In front of them the Cliff Road straightened out, and it was a clear shot to the top of Farm Hill and the dark, snowy countryside beyond.

The car slowed momentarily when the driver shifted gears. "This is my street, thanks so much." Lucille started to open the door.

"C'mon, toots." The boy beside her pulled his arm up and put it around her and smiled again with his red-hot breath three inches from her face. "We can take this jalopy on the highway to paradise."

"Let her go, Lew. She don't know what you're talking about," said the driver in the fedora; he stopped the car and Lucille twisted her body out the door, almost falling on her knees. She ran, with her galoshes flapping, along the slippery sidewalks of Argonne Drive. When she pushed open the front door of their bungalow, her father was standing in the hall with a concerned expression on his face, holding the column of the telephone with the receiver up to his ear.

"Oh my lands, well here she is, so it must be all right. Thank you, though. Thanks again." He held the receiver toward Lucille and said, "It's Naomi. She thought you got in a car with some rough customers."

"Hello." Lucille took the phone with a sob. Her whole body loosened. She looked down and saw that the palm of her right glove was covered with a red, gummy substance. It was the crimson dye for the silver slippers, crushed into a paste as red as blood.

Naomi did go to see *Rain* with Luther Russell, and she went lots of other places with him as well. He had gone back up the river to teach in the town he came from, but he came down most weekends, which gave his dating Naomi the quality of an important occasion that it seemed irrelevant to object to; it would be like objecting to Sunday.

Lucille spent several uncomfortable evenings double-dating

with Naomi and Luther, with Chauncey Kincaid as her beau. She liked Luther no better than she had before. He was cold and sarcastic, and all her attempts to be nice and funny fell on stony ground. When she tried to implicate him in little jokes against the others he looked at her, she said, "as though he were smelling a bad smell."

"It is so *funny*, so funny, that Luther thinks he's getting my goat, and I just don't care," Lucille told Ruby, but she was wrong on both counts. Luther *was* getting her goat, and it was he who didn't care.

The double-dating fell away, and Lucille and Naomi continued to see each other through the weekdays when Luther was teaching at Brady's Bend. They avoided talking about him at any length between themselves, although Naomi, with a sort of defensive force in her voice, dropped his name into the conversation. ("When Luther was driving back to Brady's Bend last Sunday night, he hit a groundhog on the road. . . .")

Lucille was rather seriously dating Chauncey Kincaid at the time, but she found herself thinking more about Naomi and Luther than about the ins and outs of her own jog-along romance.

Then, one evening when once again Lucille and Naomi were standing at the foot of the cement steps, Naomi brought out, "Well, Luther asked me last weekend to marry him."

"What did you say?"

"I said I would."

Lucille felt the icy clamping of her heart that seemed to shut out most possibilities for her. She waited for only a few seconds, knowing that Naomi was looking at her.

When she had heard Freddy McFadden with his fancy ways say "Felicitations" to Ruby on her anniversary and looked it up in Emily Post, she found out that you offered a woman felicitations because congratulations implied that she had engineered her romance. With a smile, Lucille said, "Felicitations."

"Is that all you have to say?"

"No," Lucille swallowed, "Naomi dear, I'm so glad." And she leaned over and kissed her.

In the next few weeks Lucille talked brightly and a little too often to her family about Naomi's engagement. Now it was she who brought Luther's name into the conversation, and now it was she who told funny and endearing things he did, although she was hard pressed there.

She also talked a lot about Chauncey Kincaid and she was very affectionate to him on their dates.

Finally she decided she would do something nice for Naomi. She invited the Gang, including Naomi's sister Nadine, who wasn't really a member of the Gang anymore since she had gone to keep books at the tin mill, and Chauncey Kincaid's sisters, Charlotte and May, to a surprise party to celebrate Naomi's engagement. It was to be for girls only on Friday night between bridge-club weeks. Naomi had dropped out of bridge club because Luther Russell came down from Brady's Bend on Friday evening, arriving in town about 7:30, and then and Saturday were the only nights Naomi could see him.

"Are you sure Naomi can come to a party on Friday?" asked Ruby, not wanting Lucille to be hurt. But Lucille answered glibly, "Oh, Friday's the best night, 'cause there's no school the next day and everybody has dates on Saturday. Naomi can come this once."

After she had asked everybody else, she asked Naomi if she could come up and help her hem her new raspberry crepe dress for the Easter Cotillion at the Junior Women's Club. It was the shoes for this dress she had bought the dye for that evening Naomi first told her she was going out with Luther.

"I can't do it on Friday," said Naomi. "That's when Luther comes to town."

"Can't you come earlier in the evening?" Lucille pleaded.

"Why can't Ruby help you? She's a better sewer than I am."

"Oh, just come up for a little while early in the evening."

"Well, I'll see but I really doubt it."

"Just for a little while . . ."

For the whole week before the party, Lucille's heart sang. She bought pretty crepe paper baskets of pink and yellow and green— springtime colors—and mints to put in them, and she bought a beautiful luncheon set of tablecloth and napkins with lace insertion at Wainwright's to give Naomi as an engagement present— her own present to Naomi, not from the Gang.

What she did not do, prompted by some superstitious corner of her mind, was call Naomi to check about the supposed sewing date.

Friday evening came and everyone arrived at seven o'clock. It was an hour earlier than bridge club began, but Lucille wanted to be sure that everybody got there before Naomi.

Just before supper she had finally called Naomi and said, "You're coming up to help me sew tonight, aren't you?" And Naomi had answered, "I'll have to see what train Luther's on."

At 7:30 Naomi had not appeared. All the girls in the Dinsmores' living room chatted in bright little gusts, as disheveling to good spirits as the March wind outside was to hairdos. May Kincaid stood in the kitchen door talking to her old friend Ruby who, with an apron on, was playing a mother this evening, not a hostess. "She's sure got a taste for knickknacks. . . ." Ruby's voice came strong into one of the silences that fell on the group more and more often.

Then Charlotte Kincaid, who was always nervous, knocked one of the crepe paper baskets off the edge of an end table and the mints and jellybeans hit the floor with a malicious clatter, sprinkled with Charlotte's little shrieks.

"I guess I better call Naomi," said Lucille apologetically. "She may have gotten mixed up about the time."

Her brow was furrowed like that of a child who is about to dive into water she doesn't know the depth of when she picked up the telephone and gave Naomi's number to the operator. Mrs. Vogel answered and said, "Yes, just a minute, Lucille, she's here." When Naomi came on, Lucille said, "Are you coming up here for a while?"

Naomi said, "I can't. I'm sorry, Luther got here on an earlier train."

"Well, honey, it's not really to help me sew; I'm having a party."

"I'm sorry." Naomi sounded like Lucille had told her she was having a dish of alphabet soup.

"But, honey, it's a party for *you*. It's a surprise party. An engagement party."

"I'm sorry. I told you I couldn't come if Luther was here." Naomi's voice seemed perfectly calm.

"Oh Naomi." Lucille tried to keep her voice from trembling. "Couldn't you come for just a little while? Everybody's here," she said. "We've got presents for you."

"I'm sorry."

"Luther could come."

"No." There was silence. "Thank you, though. Good-bye." The line went dead.

THE ANKLE
BRACELET

M Y mother was always quite mean about her cousin Jane. Six years older than Jane, Lucille was a flapper, and preserved into old age a taste for curls, ruffles, bracelets, and beestung Cupid's-bow lips. Jane was the 1930s version; same high forehead and fine features but she wore her hair in a lank pageboy curl, wore shirtwaist dresses—cotton for day, silk for evening—and no makeup. "Jane always had more money than I," Mother would say, "but I was prettier."

The one incongruous thing about Jane was that she wore an ankle bracelet—a thin chain of gold beneath her stocking. I remarked on this when I was quite young (I was a snobbish little boy, as only children often are) because I knew that only girls who worked in the five-and-dime wore ankle bracelets. But my mother, relenting on that one point, would say, "Oh, that's just Jane. Everybody's allowed to wear one wrong thing."

When I was an adult, eking out a precarious living as a writer in New York City, the widowed Jane moved into a retirement home near Pittsburgh so that she could be near my mother. That was when I came to know her well and hear all the stories about her. Jane and my mother had grown up together in Parnassus, and when our ancestors had come down out of the hills to work in—and with any luck own—the mines and mills that gouged the river valleys, there was enough money to live nicely, as they said, and once in a while somebody had just barely missed the right vein of coal. Certainly in our family there was more working in the mills than owning them, but Aunt Hallie, Cousin Jane's mother, used to say, "Now your great-grandmother's half-sister, Bess Blue, married one of old Judge Mellon's brothers—but that was before they had their money."

Aunt Hallie and Uncle Lawndis and Jane had themselves not done too badly. Uncle Lawndis had started as an office boy at Standard Sanitary Company—familiar to this day to every man in America because across the back of most public urinals (which one regards in an enforced moment of contemplation) are scrolled in blue Baroque letters the words *American Standard*. By the 1920s Uncle Lawndis had risen to become a vice-president at Standard, had lunch at the Duquesne Club, and had built a big square house for Aunt Hallie and Jane on one of the fine old streets down by the park along the Pennsylvania Railroad tracks.

In terms of Parnassus, Pennsylvania, the Hamiltons had made it.

After my mother's mother died and her father remarried, she, like a pretty, poor Jane Austen heroine, was farmed around to various aunts. Spirited, flirtatious, and competitive, she shared a bedroom for long periods in her youth with Jane, who was lazy, sensual, and beautiful.

Two marks of Aunt Hallie's status in town were that she always had a maid, black Lena, and diamond earrings. One year there was a popular song called "Everyone Cheers When Mama Appears, 'Cause She's Got Diamonds Stuck in Her Ears," and years later my mother would sing it, pursing her painted lips— slashed now with wrinkles—as she must have pursed them when she danced around the Victrola in Aunt Hallie's rich, somber parlor.

Everyone cheers when Mama appears
'Cause she's got diamonds stuck in her ears,
But poor Papa, poor Papa,

He's got nothin' at all.
Christmas comes and Mama gets the most expensive frocks
Papa gets a necktie and a pair of ten-cent socks!
Oh, everyone cheers, etc, etc.

Now Jane, who was mostly silent between her mother's con-stant pointed chatter ("I always said if Lawndis was fool enough to get me diamond earbobs, I'd be fool enough to get m'ears pierced to wear 'em.") and my mother's insinuating sweet chat-ter, nonetheless had a mind of her own. When she went away to boarding school she came back smoking cigarettes, for instance. But the reason she had been sent to boarding school in the first place was far more inflammatory than that: She had fallen in love with an Italian boy.

Johnny Vitale was the son of old Rocco Vitale, who owned the newsstand by the World War I monument where Main Street turned toward River Street. Old Rocco had black curls, few teeth, and a big belly, which showed when he sat outside the newsstand in summer wearing only trousers and an undershirt. Ladies like Aunt Hallie raised fluttering fingers after they passed him and wondered what the town was coming to; girls like Lu-cille and Jane avoided him altogether. He had wandering hands.

Johnny, who inherited his father's black curls with the creamy skin and blue eyes of the northern Italian, had refined his father's lust into pure electric charm. He was short—"little piss-ant dago," Uncle Lawndis once called him—and a bit stocky, but he was never still enough for you to notice. In Parnassus High School, where everybody but he and Petey Sabetta was named McLaughlin, McClellan, Hamilton, or Stewart, he had streaked in and plucked, with the ease of picking a bunch of fine Italian grapes, the captainship of the football team and the presidency of the senior class. When he sat in school wearing one of the sleeveless pullovers knitted in bright zigzags that were the fashion then, he seemed to crackle with energy.

Jane and he had begun to notice each other in tenth grade and in eleventh grade he asked her to a school party. They were somewhat limited because Jane wasn't allowed to go out on dates alone with a boy, and she couldn't invite him to church functions, needless to say. Then one Sunday he appeared, with his curls plastered down with water, in the Hamilton pew in the Parnassus Presbyterian Church with Uncle Lawndis looking like a thundercloud and Aunt Hallie wearing a "just you *dare* say anything" look toward the rest of the congregation. That Sunday Jane looked self-contained as always, neither pleased nor miserable. She had a full figure and a slightly pouty mouth with a mole on her lower lip toward the center of the pout.

That was in October. In January of 1929 Jane went away to Haddon Hall in Greensburg, the county seat, for the second semester of her junior year in high school. When she came home for the summer, Uncle Lawndis sent Aunt Hallie and Jane to stay for six weeks at the St. Elmo Hotel at Chautauqua, New York, on Chautauqua Lake. The next year Jane was sent to Haddon Hall again for her last year of boarding school.

But in between times, during the weeks of Christmas vacation and those lush green weeks in June when the sycamore trees along the strip of grass beside the railroad track shivered in the little puffs of air from the river breeze, Johnny Vitale would come calling. He always wore perfectly creased trousers and perfectly polished shoes. "Fella dresses like a gentleman," Uncle Lawndis would reluctantly admit, but Aunt Hallie said, "He's nothing but a mule in horse harness. Besides, I never trust a man whose shoes are too shiny," and she looked with a guffaw, tucking her first chin into her second, at Uncle Lawndis's rather powdery brown-and-white summer wing tips.

When Johnny came Uncle Lawndis and Aunt Hallie, if they were on the porch, would say, "Just ring the bell and go on in," or if they were inside (June evenings are sometimes a little cool with a tang in the air), Aunt Hallie or Lena would answer the door and call upstairs, "Jane, Johnny's here." And then they left him standing in the hall.

The hall in that house was square and the stairs came down along the back wall to a landing three steps from the floor. There was a sort of screen of vertical spindles of golden oak between the stairs and the hall—like a railing going all the way to the ceiling. While Johnny stood not awkwardly but alone in the hall, he could see Jane in her white dress come down behind the screen like a princess from a tower. She never spoke to him until she got to the landing, and sometimes not until she was standing in front of him in the hall. She usually would just say, "Hello there," and smile her lazy smile. Girls in those days wore summer dresses with short sleeves tight around their upper arms, and Jane's arms, which were smooth and white, blushed up to where the sleeves cut into the plump flesh.

My mother said, "I know she was in love with him. I was standing in the parlor once when she came down the stairs to meet him. She just blushed rose color all over, even her arms."

The interesting thing about these two, apparently, was that they were in a world of their own. He concentrated all that energy on her. He was focused on her like he was focused when he saw a break in the other team's line on the football field, or when Miss McLaughlin was explaining trigonometry to the few people who signed up to take it. He was absorbed by her, but he wasn't deferential. She wasn't really a princess coming down from her tower behind the golden oak screen for him, she was just, completely, Jane Hamilton—and that was enough.

After she graduated from Haddon Hall, Jane was sent to Hood College in Maryland, which somebody had impressed on Aunt Hallie as the acme of gentility. My mother six years before had gone to the state teachers' college over in the next county, and Aunt Hallie herself had never considered going to college at all. Johnny Vitale began laboriously but buoyantly to attend such classes as he could afford at the University of Pittsburgh, known as Pitt. Alternate semesters he would work wherever he could, sometimes working in the steel mills in the summer. During those summers his skin acquired a permanent blush reflecting the heat of the molten steel and his muscles grew hard. He lost his look of a black-haired cherub, and beneath his zigzag sleeveless sweaters and the white shirts, his shoulders rippled smoothly when he sat—always straining forward—in one of Aunt Hallie's massive overstuffed chairs.

Jane, after one year at Hood, announced she was homesick and she was transferring to Pitt. Aunt Hallie raged and said, "All right then, missy, if you won't go where's good for you, you don't need to go any place a'tall. You can just stay right here at home and get a job at the aluminum company for fifteen dollars a week." But Uncle Lawndis gave her the money to enroll at Pitt and bought her a little blue Buick coupe. Four mornings a week, Jane, wearing her coat with the fox collar and a tam on the side of her sleek head, picked up Johnny Vitale with a raucous honking in front of the newsstand and rolled off to the city.

After a month of this, Aunt Hallie announced at Sunday dinner that she had been talking to Mrs. Evans, the wife of the church janitor, a depressed woman who had come, as they said, from "nice people" and whose old drunk husband had dragged her down. "That poor Mrs. Evans has such a hard time with that old coot of a husband, he drinks don'cha know, and she's got some money together from her sister to send their Lewie to college. Well, he's going in on the train and that's just more money they have to spend, so I said, 'Now that's just a piece of foolishness, Jane here and Johnny Vitale go in every day in Jane's car and there's plenty of room for three.' "

The next morning Jane picked up Lewie Evans after she picked up Johnny Vitale. Whether Aunt Hallie had realized that three sit closer in a one-seat coupe than two, nobody knew.

In the spring Johnny had to drop out again and work, but he went in to night school on the train, and Jane stayed those evenings—"to study in the library"—and drove him home. Once they didn't get home until midnight, instead of ten as they were supposed to, and Uncle Lawndis, stirred to action, took Jane's car keys away for a month himself. Then she took the train.

Through all of this Jane remained serene, luscious as a peach, and eager to please. The days when she wasn't going to stay late and study, she always said as she went out the door, "I'll be home as soon as ever I can, Mama." Johnny acquired more polish every month, opening doors for Jane and stepping quickly around to the curb side when he and she walked up Sixth Avenue to go to the movies. His essential quality of contagious energy was not diminished by his new manners. When he came in the house you just felt the sun had come out, my mother said. Even Aunt Hallie would give grim smiles, tucking her chins into one another, when he was in the parlor.

Then at the end of Jane's sophomore year, the semester when Johnny had to work, one Friday night he gave her a little blue velvet box. Inside was a fine gold-chained ankle bracelet with a little plaque with *Jane* and *John* and the date *5/32* on it.

Nobody knew exactly what that meant, and in that house, like the good Presbyterians they were, they never talked about it. Whether it was a promise for the future or a commemoration of a consummation too awful to think of remained Jane's secret. He must have said in that purring burr of a voice, "This is for you, babe," but how he felt and how she felt only they and every lover in the world knew. What it *was*, however, appalled the family almost as much as what it *meant*. Aunt Hallie's least scathing response was to say when she could get her breath back—and then repeat for weeks afterwards, "Rings on her fingers and bells on her toes, she shall have music wherever she goes!"

That summer she took Jane off to Chautauqua a whole week before the season even began up there.

Now while Aunt Hallie had been protecting Jane at Chautauqua, all was not quiet at home. Uncle Lawndis in his youth had been a member of the semiprofessional Parnassus Home Runners baseball team. He had kept a broad grin, snapping brown eyes, and a lean body. While Aunt Hallie over the years developed a bust as formidable as her sharp tongue, Uncle Lawndis eased into the role of a small-town ladies' man. There had been a flirtation with a foolish maiden schoolteacher on the next block and some cheerful courtesies observed with secretaries on the commuters' train. Uncle Lawndis liked family life—apart from Aunt Hallie's sharpness—and liked to live as the pillar of the community that he was, so there was never too much danger.

But then Aunt Hallie started to take Jane to Chautauqua, and at the same time a new secretary appeared at Standard Sanitary with the provocative name of Lillie Lord.

Provocative her name and provocative her nature, apparently. She and Uncle Lawndis were seen having lunch several times in Pittsburgh restaurants, and the fact was reported by ill-meaning gossips to Aunt Hallie. Then, more damningly, a woman fresh up from Parnassus sat herself down next to Aunt Hallie in the row of rocking chairs on the St. Elmo veranda and remarked that "it was a shame Mr. Hamilton was working so hard, why sometimes he had to get the very last train out of the city at twelve o'clock at night." The next week Aunt Hallie and Jane went home.

Through the rest of that summer and into the fall, things continued to progress in an outwardly tranquil manner. Johnny showed up every Friday night, pants creased sharp enough to cut butter, and squired Jane off to the Marx Brothers or *Gold Diggers of 1932* (which made Aunt Hallie snort), and on Saturday nights they went to parties at one or another of their friends'. From Pittsburgh there occasionally came rumbles of Uncle Lawndis and Lillie Lord having lunch, but he stepped off the 6:05 on the dot every evening and walked up the promenade under the sycamore trees to his house.

Just before a family dinner on Labor Day, Johnny Vitale asked to speak to Uncle Lawndis. At dinner—to which he had been invited—he announced that he had asked Jane for her hand in marriage, she had accepted, and they hoped to be married at Thanksgiving.

Now it is at this point that the story gets murky. My grandfather was down on his luck—as happened to him from time to time—and my mother was staying at Aunt Hallie's for one of her long visits. My mother was a wonderful raconteur: places, people's expressions, details of clothing and furniture, even the weather, leaped out of her anecdotes. The only thing was that her people came so complete that you never questioned whether she, often a leading character herself, might have interpreted others' motives with a particular slant favorable to herself.

At any rate, she said that when Johnny made his announce-
ment, Aunt Hallie just barked out "*No!*" and Uncle Lawndis
said, "We'll talk about this later." Aunt Hallie's fingernail
scratched across the double damask tablecloth so it sounded like
chalk on a blackboard.

Jane cried for a week and then they compromised that they
would be married when she graduated. If she went to summer
school she could finish by a year from Christmas.

But in October it all blew up. Old Rocco Vitale got cancer
and Johnny had to quit school and his part-time job keeping
books in the steel mill to work in the newsstand and take care of
his father.

Then one afternoon Mother came home from standing on her
feet all day teaching second grade and walked into the middle of
a storm. She opened the door into that square front hall with the
golden oak screen across the back wall and shook her umbrella
slightly. It was a gray drizzly day with leaves stuck like wet newspaper to the slate sidewalks of the old town. Murky light, which
obscured rather than illuminated, filled every corner of the hall
like fog.

"Lucille?" Aunt Hallie's voice came hoarse and peremptory
from the parlor. Mother walked into the parlor, but there were
no lights on and for a moment she couldn't see Aunt Hallie.
Then she saw her sitting in her prized wing chair, covered in oys-
ter satin, bought new from Horne's last Christmas, in which nobody ever sat but company and certainly not a member of the
family on a rainy Tuesday afternoon. Aunt Hallie was holding
her head propped on her hand. "Do you know where this came
from?" She held out a folded piece of white letter paper to
Mother.

As my mother took the paper from Aunt Hallie, she said,
Aunt Hallie's pince nez glittered, and it looked as though there
were tears behind the glasses but surely not, because she had
never seen Aunt Hallie cry. She walked over to the window to
read the letter and saw the blue swirling letterhead of Jos. Horne
Co. at the top. The letter said that Horne's would be happy to

open an account in the name of Mr. Lawndis Hamilton, separate from the account in the name of Mrs. Lawndis Hamilton, and that billing would be sent to his attention at the American Standard Company, 625 Grant Street, Pittsburgh, Pa.

"It was on the hall table. There was no envelope. It must've fallen out of Lawndis's briefcase and somebody picked it up," Aunt Hallie said.

"I guess so." Mother was uncertain.

"Well," Aunt Hallie drew a deep sigh, "if Lawndis Hamilton wants a separate account at Horne's, he can have a separate account and a separate life, but he'll have a separate wife too, because he'll not do it with me." She stood up, gripped her girdle, pulled it down, and straightened her skirt. "There's no light in here, you can't see your hand in front of your face." She twitched the chain of the bridge lamp behind the wing chair, said "You've tracked leaves in all over the rug," and stalked out of the room.

Dinner that evening was conducted in glacial silence, although Uncle Lawndis, ignorant on the one hand, and Jane, innocent on the other, just thought Aunt Hallie was having a spell. After dinner, when Lena had cleared away the dessert plates with the remains of the butterscotch banana-cream pie, Aunt Hallie said, "Jane, I'll share one of your cigarettes this evening."

Aunt Hallie occasionally smoked in a rather defiant puffing way, and it usually betokened a domestic crisis.

"Well, this is a change," said Uncle Lawndis mildly.

"The first of many," said Aunt Hallie, holding the cigarette up between two fingers like a flag signaling a change in the wind. "Lawndis, I want to speak to you upstairs."

Jane and my mother drifted back to the sun parlor behind the dining room, where Jane turned on the radio for *Fibber McGee and Molly* and draped herself over the wicker couch with her schoolbooks. Mother, after an interval, went upstairs to the bathroom. She lingered outside Uncle Lawndis and Aunt Hallie's bedroom door as long as she safely could, and she heard Aunt Hallie say in burning tones, "You can make a fool of yourself and neglect me, but you're not going to neglect your child. I want you to do something about Jane and that little dago." There was a murmured response and Aunt Hallie said, "What can you do? You can give him a job. He'd do anything to get ahead. Give him a job down at Standard on the condition he break things off with Jane. Otherwise, he'll never get out of that newsstand, and what's more, Jane will be in there with him. Is that what you want? Your daughter running Rocco Vitale's filthy crummy newsstand?"

Mother crept back downstairs.

The next few weeks were hell in the Hamilton household. Uncle Lawndis became completely taciturn, while Aunt Hallie talked more than ever and always in sharp, wise-cracking tones that caught the listener like splinters in bare feet. ("When I was a girl I was taught blind obedience and no daughter of mine eats my food and then talks back to me.")

She also became nasty to my mother. "I guess Lucille can't help her father this month since she spent all her money on a new hat and purse. Charity must not be such bitter bread as the Bible says 'tis. . . ."

"I *was* helping my father," my mother would tell years afterwards. "I sent him a third of every paycheck. The Hamiltons were jealous because I was always popular and had a lot of beaux and Jane never did. I didn't want to live there, although Aunt Hallie was darling to me at first, but I had no choice. Daddy had lost his job and had to go out and live at the Farm, and I couldn't get in from the Farm to teach, and it was all just awful. Aunt Hallie wouldn't take any money from me for my room and board—it got so I could hardly stand it."

After two weeks Jane's eyes were so swollen she could hardly see. Then late one Saturday afternoon Uncle Lawndis stopped by the newsstand and took Johnny out for a drive. Nobody knew what passed between them, but within a month Johnny had begun to work at American Standard.

For a week after Uncle Lawndis and Johnny had their talk, nothing unusual happened between Jane and Johnny. Then, after their customary Friday night date, Jane had come home sobbing so desperately that she woke my mother up when she came into their shared bedroom. "He says he can't see me any-more. He said, 'Baby, I gotta do this or I'll be in that newsstand forever. It'll just be for a year, and then when I've got enough money saved up and my pop is better, I'll get a job someplace else. Besides, your dad will like me better when I've done good at work.'" Jane threw herself on her bed, her coat with the fur col-lar slipping off one shoulder. "But it doesn't matter whether Daddy likes him or not, it's Mama, and she'll never like him."

So that was it. And furthermore that was Jane's only outburst. In that family the only person who let feelings show was Aunt Hallie, and with her it was a case of taking aim before she let fly. Over the next six weeks Jane's looks deteriorated. Her opalescent skin lost its glow and became just white, and she sort of drooped and sagged all over.

She still drove into school, only now it was just with Lewie Evans.

Predictably, she and Lewie Evans began to date after six months or so. It was along about the same time that Johnny's fa-ther died and he sold the newsstand and moved to Pittsburgh— "so he wouldn't have to commute."

And, predictably, after a long courtship during which Jane was more languid and aloof than ever, she and Lewie Evans got mar-ried. Aunt Hallie had broken up one of Jane's attempts at mar-riage; either she didn't have the nerve or the interest to try again. Lewie Evans went on to become vice-president of sales for West-inghouse. "He did real well," my mother always said. "Jane lived all over the United States," she would point out, as though that were a career in itself.

But the general feeling was voiced, repeatedly over the years, by Aunt Charlotte on my father's side of the family who raised her eyebrows to murmur, "I always thought Jane Hamilton could have done a little bit better than Lewie Evans."

In her old age, when Jane was a widow, she moved to St. George's, a new retirement home near Pittsburgh.

"You'll be amused at Saint George's," the wife of a high school friend I ran into during the Christmas holidays told me. "They put up these concrete slabs out in the middle of a field and inside they've made an instant old Waspy club."

Linda, the woman who told me this, was beautiful, raven haired and tempestuous. We said she was Italian, which meant that, like Johnny Vitale, her parents or grandparents had been immigrants and her father worked in a mill. It also meant that except to comment on her figure, we had hardly noticed her in high school. It was a real tribute to the persistent imagination of handsome, conventional Spencer (aka "Buster") Brown, my high school classmate, that he married her.

"Buster's Aunt Emily is at Saint George's and she just loves it," Linda had said. "The old ladies get dressed up a million times a day and have tea parties before dinner and everybody there belongs to the Presbyterian Church." Her voice fell, and she shivered a little bit as crowds of Christmas shoppers swirled around us. "It gives me the creeps."

The day after Christmas we went to visit Jane and took her out for a drive. I drove, my father bundled up in his overcoat sitting beside me in the front seat, my mother hectic and animated as ever in the back beside Jane, who snuggled her cheek into her fox collar. We went up and down and around the thrusting little hills that corrugate Western Pennsylvania. Leafless apple orchards threw patterns like wire sculpture across the winter fields.

Jane had invited us back to lunch at St. George's. It was a series of raw brick and concrete apartment buildings with ugly balconies that looked like folded cardboard. Indoors, however, it was quite different. Linda Carelli Brown had been absolutely right. The hallways had dark paneling up to a chair rail and golden flocked wallpaper. It looked like Aunt Hallie's Parnassus house. There was the comforting musty smell of overheated dry wood that had permeated my childhood winters.

In her boxy apartment Jane slipped out of her coat and, pointing to the couch, said, "Sit ye down until it's time for lunchers." We talked while Jane puffed on her cigarette, held stiffly as usual between plump white, red-tipped fingers. We spoke of Buster and

Linda's Aunt Emily, whom Jane said laconically that she knew—
"a nice enough person."

While we talked, Jane sat on a straight chair, which belonged
to her little dining room table, and she sat hunched into herself,
her legs crossed, swinging one ankle. Beneath her sheer nylon
stocking the anklet bracelet still glittered, brightly elusive as pas-
sion itself, around her leg.

Jane spoke of her mother, Aunt Hallie. "After Daddy got so
bad, became 'senile,' as they call it now"—Jane wrinkled her
nose and pulled in her chin in a good imitation of her mother
at the crassness of modern terms and times—"well, Mama just
didn't go out. She hadn't gone anywhere except to the hairdresser and the bank for eighteen years when he died. Neither of
them went to Pittsburgh one single time from the day he retired."
Jane and my mother shook their heads sorrowfully together. "He
just didn't seem to want to leave her," said Jane.

After lunch—chicken à la king and a salad in St. George's
processed antique dining room—we retrieved our coats from
Jane's apartment. She and my mother kissed each other with
little pecks on the lips and we left.

On the way home I said, "So Uncle Lawndis didn't want to
leave Aunt Hallie in the end."

"Well," said Mother, "he was out of his mind, wasn't he?" After she had given a bark of a laugh, she said, "Oh, even when he
could have, I don't think he wanted to. Anyway, Aunt Hallie always won."

Then she said, "I loved Aunt Hallie. She could be mean, but I
loved her. And you know, when I lived there, everybody, just
everybody who didn't know us well, thought that I was her
daughter and Jane was her niece. I looked so much like her that
when I would go upstreet on Saturday afternoon to shop, people
would say to Aunt Hallie, 'We saw your daughter this afternoon,'
and she would say, 'No, that was my niece,' and they would say,
'But she looks just like you,' and she would say, 'My niece does
look like me. She's more like me than my own daughter.'"

Mother said with a sharp twist in her voice, "Jane was such a stick-in-the-mud."

A sudden terrible thought occurred to me. I asked, "How did the separate Horne's charge notice get left on the hall table so that Aunt Hallie saw it?"

"I put it there," said my mother.

"Why?"

"I thought she should know. It wasn't right."

"But that was how Aunt Hallie got Uncle Lawndis to get Johnny Vitale away. That was how Aunt Hallie blackmailed him."

My mother said calmly, with the serenity born of a lifetime of self-delusion, "I didn't know that was what she'd do. Anyway, Johnny Vitale wasn't right for Jane. He was just using her."

"But she loved him," I said rather desperately.

"Apparently," my mother chuckled. The hills dipped and swirled outside the car windows in the failing December afternoon while the night deepened like the past itself.

INTERLUDE

A Meditation upon the Pursuit of Happiness

Pᴀʀᴛɪᴇꜱ for older people seemed to me to be grand state affairs when I was small, something like church. Aunt May and Aunt Charlotte, their friend Maisie McCreight, Ruby and my mother, and three other friends had a bridge club that met every other Friday night. ("Those people were old enough to be my mother. Well, in fact one of them *was* my mother," said my mother.) Bridge club was distinguished by competitive desserts (one confection I particularly remember included mandarin oranges and coconut folded into whipped cream in a ring of ladyfingers. The exotic names were a fascination in themselves—that concoction was known as ambrosia. But it didn't count as company dessert unless the ladyfingers were homemade. "It took her hours and hours to make," was an essential part of a favorable judgment for any contender).

The club's advent at one's own house was heralded by a thorough house cleaning, then getting out the card tables and chairs, placing the card-table covers, the scorecards, new pencils, dishes of nuts and candy, and finally the great evening arrived when the doorbell rang and the ladies all swept in in clumps with shrieks and hoots of laughter, snow frosting their hats and fur collars. Little courtier that I was, I knelt and took off their galoshes for them, and then they progressed upstairs to put their coats on the twin beds in Mother and Father's room (he, reading his paper and smoking his cigar in the rocking chair in the guest room, waved amiably at the ladies, who poked their heads in and appreciatively whiffed the male aura). In the bedroom the ladies engaged in mysterious rites such as rouging their cheeks, and one of them showed me how the scarlet polish on her nails carefully arched above the "moon" at the base of the nail. Long after I was in bed, from the stairwell where the light rose and faded in the upstairs hall to a glow that just touched the tip of the unaccustomed yellow blaze in my parents' room, there came a vigorous babble, topped with loud laughter, as though everyone were performing a crazy variation of a church cantata. Performing they certainly were, for each other, all at once.

Their characters, long known to each other, were revealed again at the card tables. "If Charlotte or Maisie McCreight bids, you know she has every card in the deck," they said, "but if May or Ruby bids, it's all nerve."

Sometimes there were arguments, fights! "May and Maisie McCreight got into it last night," my mother would say, which meant that there had been an exchange of a few peppery words, a shake of the head and pursing of the lips, and then someone would tell a joke and the course of the evening roared on.

Adult parties that I observed were pageants to be savored. Parties that I participated in, children's parties and then later parties for "young people"—annihilating category—were another matter.

In the first place, in Parnassus particularly, but also in the upscale suburb of Cedar Hill where we moved when I was eight, there was more than a whiff of icy Puritan disapproval of any levity that was a product of alcohol or just the intoxication that came from contact between youngsters of opposite sexes. Within my grandfather's memory, people had been "sessioned"—called up before the church congregation and publicly reprimanded—for dancing. And rich cousin Jane Hamilton reminisced about a New Year's Eve dance at the country club in the 1930s (my mother ground her teeth; her family had not belonged to the country club) when the young people sat around in evening dresses and dinner jackets conversing until midnight because New Year's Eve fell on a Sunday and they couldn't dance until after the clock struck twelve.

Every church in the up-and-coming Pittsburgh suburb where my parents and I lived was Presbyterian except for one that was Episcopalian. The junior high school was named for Andrew W. Mellon, and most of the men in the community worked for either U.S. Steel or Alcoa. It was a place of great rectitude.

Nonetheless, there were distinctions. My parents were schoolteachers, respected but not included—particularly not in the cocktail parties given in the big houses over in Neville Manor where the hard-working executives' wives expended tremendous care twice a year or so to ape what they thought was the high life. And the churches were subtly different, one from another. Our Presbyterian church was a huge gray stone building with two towers, Gothic in style, chilly both in atmosphere and doctrine. An assistant minister who had come there from California, a kindly, sad-faced man in his fifties, said that although he had enjoyed smoking a pipe when he came to Cedar Hill, he discovered that none of the other ministers on the staff did so and he felt it was better to put his aside. Not that this would avail him anything in the cosmic long run: "By Faith are ye Saved, Not Works lest any man should Boast" was often the text for a sermon.

The other big church in town—big in size and big in influence—was also Presbyterian; named the Westminster Presbyterian Church, it was where society people went. The president of the Westinghouse Corporation went there; most of the U.S. Steel executives went there, and while it was sure as shootin' that the congregation drank, as we said through thin lips, it was even suspected that the ministers raised a glass in the right company. The manse for that church was a pleasant white clapboard house with black shutters. It had been built in the 1920s for the first minister of the church; next door to it, in fact only about ten feet away, there was a much smaller replica, white clapboard, black shutters, but only two windows wide instead of six, erected for that first minister's black help, whom he brought with him from the South.

This church even held dances for the young people on Friday nights. By my day they had turned the house for the black help into a recreation hall, and in some vague acknowledgment of the suspect connotations of what they were doing, that was where the dances were held.

Ultimately, the differences between the two churches were more cosmetic than real, however. One Sunday when I was a child I attended the Westminster Church with a friend's family, and there heard the courtly soft-faced preacher rail against the crowds lined up the afternoon before outside the local movie theater to see *From Here to Eternity* with Deborah Kerr and Burt Lancaster writhing in the surf.

If Dr. Whittaker thought it was wrong to see that movie, well then it certainly was in bad taste to do so, which was much the same thing.

I was all too alert to bad movies and just how subtle their influence could be. A couple of years later I went to see *An Affair to Remember*, also with Deborah Kerr, but this time she gets hit by a car on the way to her wedding with Cary Grant after an adulterous shipboard liaison. I came home that night and had my first wet dream.

Puzzled, I told my parents. My father gave me a responsible, minimal talk—he had told me the facts of life a year or two before in the same manner, explaining that I had now come to "man's estate." My mother said that I should understand that the woman in the movie had done something very, *very* wrong.

Neither of us had to mention that she had been crippled for life because of it.

The danger of enjoyment lurked everywhere. Girls could get pregnant, although very few did in that school, they were rewarded so thoroughly for living correctly. Boys could get maimed in a car wreck—the captain of the football team lay in a coma for six weeks in the hospital, came out a shrunken, dull version of

his handsome self, and shortly thereafter his family moved because he had to be put into a special school. And, most dangerous of all, you could just not do your homework one night too
many, not do well in school the next day on an important test,
not get into the right college, and end up living in the *wrong part
of town.*

Salvation in this life, salvation in the next—it all had to do
with being constantly on the alert for the snare of gratification.
And even then, do everything right and you could never be sure;
by Faith are ye saved, not works.

No mentor, no effort was to be trusted until the day was over,
the game won. The only guide to what was right that a person
could invoke was his own conscience—and even then it was better not to think things through but just to rely on the rules. "If
you have to ask yourself whether it's okay, then you probably
shouldn't do it," they said in Sunday school.

Priggish and precocious little historian that I was, I had
absorbed, at my grandparents' on one summer visit, a sort of lesson from a text in an old history book that seemed to me to illuminate the manipulation of conscience and the rich harrowing
of guilt that we were all prey to. *A History of the County of Westmoreland, Pennsylvania,* written in the 1880s in rich Latinate
prose by one George Albert, stood on a bookshelf in the upstairs bedroom of my grandparents' cottage. It was a massive
volume, about the size of a dictionary, bound in crumbling dark
red leather with red masking tape holding the spine together.
Aunt Charlotte and Aunt May had the same book (no masking
tape) in their junk room; it was *A History of the County of Westmoreland* that contained the story of the captivity of Massy
Harbison.

In that book, which I perused frequently, fascinated by the
stories of Indian raids and settlement of the valleys, which alter-
nated with steel engravings of bearded old men ("Judge McClung
is a prominent citizen of the community of Poke Run. . . ."),
there was the story of an influential preacher from the early days,

one Samuel Porter. I found his way of approaching things particularly instructive.

The account said:

There was a sermon given by the Reverend Mr. Porter at Congruity which was worthy of note. After 1798 the minister's spirit had consumed his body like a fire consumes a log and he became too frail to care for both Poke Run and Congruity. Therefore he agreed to remain as Pastor of Congruity in return for 120 per annum, one-half in merchantable wheat at five shillings per bushel and the remainder in cash.

While pastor there a new stone tavern had been built on the turnpike, scarcely a mile from the church, and was just opened by the owner, a very clever man. The young folks of the neighborhood had agreed to have what was generally known as a housewarming by holding a ball there. The arrangements were all made, the tickets distributed, and the guests invited. On the Sabbath previous to the intended ball Mr. Porter, after preaching an eloquent sermon sitting in his old split-bottomed armchair (For he was too feeble to preach standing, and for many a long day sat and preached in that old armchair, elevated in the pulpit for his accommodation), and before dismissing the congregation, gave out the usual notices for the ensuing week and Sabbath. He then gave notice that on the next Thursday evening, at early candle-lighting, a ball was to be held about three-fourths of a mile from that place. He said it was to be hoped that all the polite young ladies and gentlemen would attend, as it was said to be a place where politeness and manners could be learned and cultivated, and that many other things could be said in favor of attending such places which it was not necessary for him to mention at that time. He remarked that, for his part, if he did not attend, the young folks would excuse him, as it was likely he might be detained at Presbytery; yet should Presbytery adjourn in time and nothing else prevent he expected to attend, and, should he be present, he would open the exercises of the night by reading a text of Scripture, singing a psalm, and be dismissed. Then with a full and solemn voice and in the most impressive manner he read the ninth verse of the eleventh chapter of Ecclesiastes. Then he announced and read the Seventy-Third Psalm. After this was sung he offered up a fervent and affecting prayer, praying earnestly for the thoughtless and gay, and for the power of God's Spirit to guard them from those vices and amusements which might lead the youthful mind to fritter away precious time and neglect the one thing needful, and then, with his solemn benediction, the congregation was dismissed. The evening set for the ball arrived and passed away, but the ball was never held, the whole community having been loudly awakened by the venerable pastor's discourse.

Lacking the eighteenth- and nineteenth-century Calvinist's easy acquaintance with the Bible, I had to go downstairs, get Ruby's Bible from her bedside table, and return upstairs.

The verses of Psalm 73 rained down on my head with very little less effect than they had on that unsuspecting congregation duped—or, as they would say, saved—by the minister's devious and sarcastic discourse.

> [3] For I was envious at the foolish, when I saw the prosperity of the wicked. . . .
> [7] Their eyes stand out with fatness; they have more than the heart could wish. . . .
> [17] Until I went into the sanctuary of God; then I understood their end.
> [18] Surely Thou didst set them in slippery places; Thou castedest them down into destruction.
> [19] How are they brought into desolation, as in a moment! They are utterly consumed with terrors. . . .

[27] For, lo, they that are far from Thee shall perish; Thou has
destroyed all them that go a-whoring from Thee.

The whiplash of terror that penetrated the slower minds of
that old-time congregation as they realized that they had been
deliberately led astray in their hopes of merriment, and the reflections of the quicker minds as they realized that they had been
led astray as a metaphor for how easily life itself could lead them
to "neglect the one thing needful," could not have been more
terrible to them than my reflections were to me.

After what seemed a great while, I roused myself sufficiently to
look at the last passage referred to in the account of Mr. Porter's
sermon, hoping against hope for some expiation. Ecclesiastes
declaimed:

Rejoice, O young man, in thy youth; and let thy heart
cheer thee in the days of thy youth, and walk in the ways of
thine heart, and in the sight of thine eyes: but know thou,
that for all these things God will bring thee into judgement.

Aspiration and retribution, the fullness of life and punishment
for it, were the oxymoronic companions of Western Pennsylvania life.

When my mother was a little girl, her mother tied her to the
porch railing of their house on Fifth Avenue to punish her.

When she, in turn, was a young teacher she put tape across her
children's mouths if they talked when she told them to be silent.

By the time I came along it was sufficient for her to glare at me
and say, "If you do not do what I tell you, you will be *severely*
punished."

Punishment loomed large in the background, if not the fore-
ground, of our family. Although never a hand was laid on me in
anger, my father used to say rhetorically, "If there is no heaven or
hell, why behave yourself in this life?"

My father also thought he knew who was going where—and

condemned himself for exercising his opinion. "My greatest fault is that I'm too judgmental," he would say.

The Ultimate Punishment hung over our heads like a wet, black cloud, but if the threat were vague, the list of prohibitions was specific indeed: We did not drink, ladies did not smoke, we did not go to the movies or play cards on Sunday, and sex might as well have been an obscure practice engaged in only by Hottentots. The principal weapon that was employed to control one was embarrassment, the threat of being caught in inappropriate behavior. Which was why transgressions of style—e.g. ladies' smoking—could be right in there with transgressions of morality. Many of the things that seemed innocent and pleasant turned out, if you were caught at them, to be terribly wrong.

FREE SPIRITS

"Drunk," according to the scholarly Dictionary of American Slang (1960), by Harold Wentworth and Stuart Berg Flexner, is the subject of 331 slang synonyms, which is the largest number for any activity, condition, or concept, including sexual acts.
—THE AMERICANS: THE DEMOCRATIC EXPERIENCE (1974),
DANIEL J. BOORSTIN (THEN LIBRARIAN OF CONGRESS)

Some of the words for drunk in The Dictionary of American Slang are:

three sheets to the wind
tight as a tick (drum, lord, owl, goat, mink, brassiere, ten-day drunk, etc.)
boozed (first recorded 1887)
all geezed up
cock-eyed
embalmed
lit (to the gills, the guards, up)
lit up like a Christmas tree (Main Street, Times Square, Broadway, a store window, a church)
pie-eyed
bent (first recorded 1833)

half-seas over
oiled (above and this first recorded 1737)
pixilated
shellacked
stinking

In 1794 the first serious challenge to the authority of the new federal government of the United States came from the farmers of Western Pennsylvania. The Whiskey Rebellion, as it is known in the history books, was a response to a federal excise tax of approximately seven cents per gallon that was to be levied on every gallon of whiskey distilled in the United States. For the farmers of Western Pennsylvania this tax would be disastrous. The only way they could get their grain to a cash market in Philadelphia—three weeks' distance across the mountains—was to distill it into whiskey and transport it in barrels. With the new law their stills would be taxed, their whiskey would be taxed, and, most unjust of all, the trial of a man accused of evading the tax would take place in a federal court across the mountains among townsmen and Quaker aristocrats in their hypocritical fine gray broadcloth. The cost of such a trial to any accused, whether he be judged innocent or guilty, would mean that he must sell his farm to get to court.

And besides all this, the tax was insidious. It carried connotations of royal power arbitrarily exercised, of the spurred boot grinding the peasant hand. For generations in Scotland and Ireland, the English overlords wielded as their tools of authority an excise tax on fine Scotch and Irish whiskey. Even Dr. Samuel Johnson, English to the marrow of his bones and beef, in his famous dictionary published in 1755, defined the word *excise* as "a hateful tax."

The Scotch-Irish frontiersmen who had come across the waters to Western Pennsylvania to escape such abuse of power and fought the Redcoats—once and for all, they thought—did not intend to have their own countrymen assume royal prerogatives.

When John Neville, who had accepted the position of inspector of the excise in the Western counties of Pennsylvania, attempted to serve a warrant for selling whiskey, a mob of five hundred men burned his house. Before the end of the year 1794 a militia of 13,000 men, dispatched by President Washington and led by Alexander Hamilton, secretary of the treasury, and Governor Henry Lee of Virginia, came into the Pennsylvania backcountry and crushed the rebellion. There was relatively little bloodshed, but oaths of allegiance to the federal government were required in which the citizens had to promise not to "oppose the execution of the acts for raising a revenue on distilling spirits and stills," and that they would "support, as far as the law requires, the civil authority."

This Whiskey Rebellion was a complete rout of frontier independence. The tough individuality that had grown wild on the frontier would be pruned back from now on. This was when the new communities growing up were named Congruity and Unity, and as the wilderness was beaten back, congruity and unity among men were to be encouraged and sometimes even enforced. The individuality and strength of character that had assured survival earlier became a threat to a peaceful community. Free spirits—personalities as well as liquor—were to be shunned. The exuberance of youth was feared and crushed. For a people who had never left John Calvin's God very far behind them, the free gesture came to be seen for what the Bible always taught it was: the beckoning hand of the Devil.

"Your great-great-grandfather was the first man in Western Pennsylvania to throw whiskey out of his harvest fields," my Great-Aunt Myra, the family sybil, would say with a fine determination to be central to history.

"Well, you know, Roscoe drinks," Ruby would say to explain my Great-Uncle Roscoe's peculiar behavior, and then, as though it were part and parcel, "of course, he's a Democrat."

"Beer is common," my father would say when I was a child. My mother would add, "It always reminds me of some old Polish man on Second Avenue, sitting on the sidewalk in his undershirt."

Alcohol, when I was a young man growing up, was a threat. It belonged to the new immigrant peoples who were an economic threat in the mills and the mines, or it belonged to smart young people who were going way beyond the bounds that had kept their fathers safe. Those fathers—prodded by the mothers who still had no vote at the time—made Prohibition the law of the land from 1919 until 1933. Alcohol remained the magic potion that would make you other than a god-fearing Parnassus Presbyterian.

When I was quite small my mother patronized a hairdresser named Rose. Rose was Italian, and she had confected her own hair into a hive of spun platinum sugar, like the cotton candy we got on a stick at Kennywood Amusement Park during the school excursion picnic in June. Rose owned a very modern house, built out of white cinder block with windows of translucent glass block. My mother, who yearned to be modern, liked Rose. One year at Christmastime Rose invited Mother to see her Christmas tree. Mother went and she took me. The Christmas tree had been frosted all over with white artificial snow and the ornaments were all silver. It scared me. It seemed to be not at all a real Christmas tree, which should be dark green with many colored lights. Our tree at home was a real tree, and so was the one in Aunt Jessie's back parlor in Apollo, where we went to visit every Christmas night.

My mother and Rose and I sat on shiny white leather seats built against the wall on two sides of her living room.

And then Rose offered Mother a glass of wine.

Mother accepted it.

The wine was the only spot of color in the room. It was a changeable red purple, which sent out darts of light of its own, very different, more vital and alien than the reflections in the Christmas-tree lights at home. It was like light that came through the red cups with people's names on them that someone had brought back from the St. Louis Exposition of 1903 that sat on top of the china closet in Great-Aunt Myra's dining room. But those were objects. The wine was something magical. Perhaps it had been melted from red glass? It was an elixir, not a drink like milk or iced tea—or even a grown-up drink like coffee that belonged to what Father called "man's estate," and which I therefore at that age couldn't have but looked forward to someday. There was no place in the daily scheme of things for wine.

Mother drank the wine, chatting with Rose, admiring everything, while I worried about how we would get home, since Mother obviously would not be able to drive.

Imagine my surprise to find that Mother drove home perfectly well and didn't seem one bit different, although I waited for days to see some residual effect of the wine.

All the aunts and great-aunts uttered the word *drinking* in the same tone of solemn judgmental horror they used to mention theft. Drinking belonged to outcasts: It was willful. People who drank were different and, what was worse, didn't care if they were.

My Great-Uncle Roscoe was an example. He had taken out his false teeth when he retired from bookkeeping at the spring works. Since, as Ruby said, he couldn't Go Out Into Society without his teeth, he stayed home on the Farm, living with my grandparents and not going out for the last twenty years of his life. Except that every evening he drove his high old Plymouth down to Denny's Tavern at the corner for a beer—or two or three.

When Uncle Roscoe finally died in 1970, my mother said, "Some strange old man came into Proudfit's Funeral Home and went up to the coffin and said, 'Oh, Rossy, Rossy,' and he cried and cried and none of us knew who he was. Wasn't that strange?"

And Aunt May would say in her butter-wouldn't-melt-in-the-mouth way, "They used to say that Tom Bonsall was such a great friend of Roscoe's, but they used to say too that if Tom had any other friends, Roscoe was jealous." Then she would give a light malicious laugh.

Foreigners, of course, drank but they didn't know any better. That was what kept them foreigners.

And rich people (aluminum company executives, who thought they were above the law) drank. A rich lady in the Parnassus Church was an alcoholic. Her family hired a black woman to be with her all the time, and the black woman—proud as Punch, they said—would accompany the lady, tormented and pale, wearing a fur coat with the high sheltering collar turned up, to church. Sometimes the lady staggered and leaned on the black woman's arm, sometimes she simply seemed white as the negative of a photograph. And the sad thing was she didn't try to do a thing about it.

"You don't know when liquor will get a hold of you," Aunt May said. "The trouble is, you take a little bit, and then a little more, and then you can't control it."

In 1931 when the Borough of Parnassus was consolidated with the neighboring Borough of New Kensington, Parnassus was primarily residential, while the principal industries of New Kensington were: The Aluminum Company of America, The Union Spring and Carbide Company, and P. F. Murphy's tin mill. The combined population of the two boroughs was 28,000 citizens. Prohibition was the law of the land and there were no legal bars in either of the two boroughs.

By 1945, the year I was born in New Kensington's Citizens' General Hospital and celebrated as heir to a host of adoring relatives, the revenues of the aluminum plants in town had begun to falter and a large portion of the workforce was transferred to the plants in Pittsburgh.

At this time, Prohibition had been repealed for twelve years, and there were 114 commercial establishments licensed to sell liquor within the boundaries of New Kensington.

Except for Uncle Roscoe, no one in my family—on either side—ever willingly set foot in a bar. When Uncle Roscoe was old and ill and couldn't drive anymore, my grandfather, wearing his pearl gray overcoat and gray felt hat, would go into the Pennsylvania State Liquor Store on Freeport Street and buy peach brandy and beer for Uncle Roscoe. When my grandfather was too old to come to town, my father had to drive up from Pittsburgh to perform the service because, although my stepgrandmother Ruby was more than able and vigorous, my grandfather said that "no wife of his would ever set foot in a liquor store."

During Prohibition a gangland family, the Martinellis, who had done more than set foot therein—indeed they had gotten their first foothold in the world of organized crime by their efforts as bootleggers—moved from New Jersey, where they were under scrutiny from the law, to New Kensington. Over the next thirty years they established a stranglehold on the town, giving it the nickname "The Little Chicago of the East" in the nation's tabloids and contributing to the exodus of industry. They could be seen lounging about the Howard Hotel, wearing white suits and white fedora hats, just like racketeers in the movies.

Needless to say, no one in my family ever spoke to a Martinelli. When a high school football player chum of my father's became mayor of New Kensington, Father said to him, "Charlie, why don't you clear those bums out of town?" and Charlie answered, "You can't do it. When I was elected, they came to me and they said, 'Now we don't bother the decent people in this town and don't you bother us.' "

The irony was that when they were finally cleared out in the 1960s by a state government suddenly gone tough on corruption, the industry had gone too and the town became wide open to every rascal in that part of Pennsylvania, Ohio, and West Virginia. The Martinellis had kept the streets clean. In their day there was no mugging, and the sixteen-year-olds who beat up and robbed my old Aunt May, thereby ultimately causing her death, would never have made it across the Ninth Street Bridge into town.

Part Three

LUCILLE AND CHAUNCEY

CHAUNCEY

My father's favorite hymns were "The Battle Hymn of the Republic" and "Amazing Grace." His favorite movie was *Birth of a Nation*, notwithstanding that it was, as we would now say, racist; he simply liked it because he had seen it when he was fourteen years old in 1914, and it impressed him. Once my father made up his mind about something, his mind tended to stay made up. For the last twenty-seven years of his teaching career he taught his pupils *Ivanhoe*, *The Lady of the Lake*, *The Last of the Mohicans*, and *A Midsummer Night's Dream*—six weeks of reading, six weeks of grammar. Rebecca (the beautiful Jewess) and Roderick Dhu and Uncas and Bottom all frolicked through our house. Once when a young plumber, who had attended Cedar Hill High School, was working in the basement, he looked up the cellar stairs, saw my father standing at the top, and exclaimed, "*The Last of the Mohicans!*"

In Father's view too that's who he was.

We always had a beleaguered, Old World view of ourselves as the last outposts of culture—a gentleman and lady's culture—and the last of the line.

Father's sense of these things stemmed from his childhood, poverty-stricken on a tenant farm but with a memory of having

been "nice people," and in his case a notion of great privilege because he was the youngest and *spoiled*.

"Your father was always spoiled," my mother says. "His sisters
spoiled him."

There had been concern about his health from the start.

*It seems at birth nothing agreed with me and I was slowly
starving,*

he wrote to me in a short account of his life that I had asked him
to prepare when he was eighty.

*They had two of the best doctors (supposedly) from New
Kensington (then Parnassus), Dr. Wilson and Dr. McConnell,
and they finally gave up and said there was nothing more could
be done. Someone suggested a country doctor who lived in the
area by the name of Scott—a younger man. He put me on
white of egg and got me started.*

With this precarious beginning little Chauncey was, under-
standably, pampered from the git-go.

*My mother was tall and thin with skirts to her ankles, [he
wrote,] and I remember many days following her around the
house hanging on to her dress and crying because I had nothing to
do on cold winter days when the rest of the family were at school.
Even when I was six I often couldn't go because it was too cold or
too much snow. They went to Webster School—4 miles or more.*

Along with pampered went willful.

*The Logan's Ferry Church Strawberry Festival ranked next to
Christmas and we always went but on one occasion the weather
was inclement and they decided not to go. Although I was only
three or four I outvoted the others and someone hitched up the
buggy and we went.*

("Your father was always spoiled," says my mother.)

When I was small there was an old photograph that puzzled me hanging as part of an arrangement in a shadow box on our dining room wall. The shadow box was a fantastic construction of my mother's made up of an elaborate Victorian picture frame dramatically painted black and highlighted in gold that framed a pink recessed interior on which, in turn, various family photographs were placed. One of the photographs showed a belligerent, square-faced, handsome child with long, corkscrew curls to the shoulders wearing a white, beruffled dress. The child in the dress was holding the hand of a tall boy with short hair wearing an Eton collar and knickers. "That," my father said, chuckling, placing a firm forefinger on the child in the dress, "is I. Little boys wore dresses in those days until they were about six."

From the eminent bulk of his masculinity, football coach and high school principal, flashing teeth and Arrow-collar smile, he is amused.

He wrote:

The picture we have on our wall with my curls resulted from the fact that they took my brother who also had curls and I to the barber to de-curl us but either from fright of the barber or love of the curls I refused to have mine cut. When the picture came it was no good and had to be done again, hence I still had my curls and my brother didn't.

I notice on the red damask wall of the house of a Georgetown dowager whom I am interviewing in connection with my work as a journalist, a portrait of a ringletted child in a white ruffled dress. "Mr. Sargent painted that portrait of my father when he was six," says the dowager. "Little boys wore dresses in those days."

Victorian love of extending innocence—however artificially—and Victorian love of drapery combined. I am also tempted to say, from the vantage point of my life and from what I know of the strength of the women in my family and their men, whose energy evaporated as the frontier and its opportunities shrank, that keeping little boys in dresses and curls presaged the future. Perhaps that is why my mother was shocked when Aunt May put the small me into her mother's dress.

Perhaps, also, she was shocked for other reasons: May surely was making me her creature, as well as tying me to the past, with that bit of grim whimsy, and my mother was quite determined that I was to be *her* boy. My mother knew the insidious addiction engendered by small amounts of poison administered early on.

For little Chauncey, however, despite the dress, his behavior as a child was no forecast of his lack of energy in later life. He was rambunctious.

It was when we lived at the Farneth place that my brother and I played catchers through the dining room and kitchen and I tied the dining room door to the canned fruit and vegetable cupboard which stood against the kitchen wall from floor to ceiling and my brother kept pulling on the door until over came the cupboard with all the season's canning in it. I went to the cornfield and stayed until dark. I do not recall that I got any punishment except silent treatment when I returned.

This is approximately what had gone into the jars on those shelves: To harrow the earth takes two days; to water the beans in a dry summer means carrying ten buckets from the well every two days at least—a bucket, of course, must be hauled by hand from the well, the average bucketful of water weighs fifteen pounds; to hoe the beans requires fifteen hours a week, more if the season is rainy and the weeds thrive—though then, of course, you do not need to carry water from the well; in August the beans mature, if they have not been eaten by the rabbits, the squirrels, the birds, or Gyp, the farm dog, trying to cleanse his stomach from a mess of rotten barn rat he had hidden behind the feed bin. To pick the beans takes two days. To heat the water to boil the Mason jars for canning requires two stove loads of wood. To chop that wood took somebody a day and a half the previous winter. The temperature in an unshaded wooden farmhouse kitchen in August would be about ninety degrees Fahrenheit, and the wood-fueled cookstove would make it much hotter. In addition to beans, there were tomatoes, peas, pickles, beets, pears, peaches, and corn in that store cupboard.

My father's mother, she who worked so hard in that kitchen, bore the maiden name of Adams. She had come from "nice people" in West Virginia. When she first married Addison Calvin Kincaid, a gaunt tenant farmer with burning eyes, her mother cried for three days. Of the seven children she bore, the third and fourth died within two days of each other of the "membranous croup"—diphtheria. Her sister, who had come to help, carved the name of the sick little boy on the windowpane with the new diamond she had received from her fiancé. But she died a week later herself. The neighbors were afraid to come close to help, so they put food on the gateposts at the end of the lane and rang a school handbell to let the family know. My father, when asked for his mother's first name while applying for his own wedding certificate, could not remember it, but said that his father had called her "Bridget," which was what you called an Irish maid, the most hard-worked creature that anybody knew of.

While all the nation had been going West for a century, Addison Kincaid in 1907 moved his family from the succession of tenant farms in the ungiving hills of Western Pennsylvania where they had been living, south and east to the Eastern Shore of Maryland because he had heard there was good truck farming there. But the soil was as much sand as loam, the weather was of a damp, unhealthy warmness, and the family had to live for nearly a year before there would be profit from the crops. First Gyp died, retching and whining and then turning still—Who would poison an old mongrel who had only ever hunted mice in the barn and played with the little boys?—and then the old couple in the lopsided, unpainted big house down the lane—not like a lane at home in Pennsylvania, which wound invitingly around among the hills, but rather just a track, straight as a die through the sand—then this old couple, swallowing their consonants and mouthing their vowels through toothless gums as humidly and viscously as the weather, mumbled of poison, asking about the dog and watching with narrowed eyes while the little boys scuffed the sand of the lane with their copper-toed boots.

But the real poison was at the heart of the family and it could not be helped. Mother, Kate Adams Kincaid, known to her granite-hard husband with rueful affection as Bridget, often woke moaning in the night. Though she was thin and her cheeks were sunken, her belly swelled. She was forty-seven, not pregnant—praise the dear Lord—but the nausea and the pain grabbed like labor too long sustained so that birth became death. Obstruction of the bowel, the country doctor said, probing with his fingers through her nightgown. Addison went down to the barn in the night and got bran mash, heating it lovingly with water to make a purge, a laxative—the worst thing, incidentally, for appendicitis.

"Mama died of appendicitis," Aunt May used to say.

"If you ever hear a man weeping, it is a dreadful sound," my father would say. "When my mother died and they were carrying her coffin out of the house, Dad went out behind the barn and cried. It is an unnatural sound."

> When we moved back to Parnassus [Father wrote] we first lived on Linden Avenue, down by the creek at the foot of 7th Street hill. Then we moved to Main Street about three doors from Dugans' and to Fifth Avenue about three houses from the cemetery at the end of the street, then on up Fifth Avenue where we lived for some twenty years.

He is wrong. He lived there for nearly thirty years until he married, and his sisters lived there for sixty-five.

When Chauncey came back from Maryland and started to go to school in Parnassus, a big brick town school with many rooms and teachers wearing long skirts like his mother's—not country girls who had taken their teacher's certificates and were somebody's sister—and more pupils than you could keep in your mind's eye, he was too confused to say that because of the snow when he was smaller and couldn't get to school, he couldn't read

as well as an eight-year-old should read. He couldn't read at all.
So he put his head down on his desk and said he was sick. When
he was sick before, Mama had been there to make him well.

His sister Charlotte went to work at the hardware store, keeping the books, and when his sister May graduated from high
school the next year, she went to work too. And then his father
left to go to California, to get work, he said. But they never saw
him again. Once in a while a postcard, a "postal," would come
from Colorado or California or Washington state with a scrawl
saying the scenery was grand and he had work and signed *Dad*,
but never an address.

"That old man never sent those children a penny," my stepgrandmother, Ruby, would say, setting her strong jaw. "Grandpa
was the postmaster in those days and he would have known."

Despite anxieties about money ("Chauncey used to tell me he
would pray when he went to sleep at night that when he woke up
it would be Christmas and there would be enough to eat," my
mother said), and worries about school, once Chauncey got the
hang of things, he enjoyed himself. He fooled around with his
friends Dag Maglisco and Ruddy Park and he laughed and told
jokes and he grew to be very, very handsome.

> *My happiest days in growing up in Parnassus* [he wrote] *were
> when I was in high school and played football and basketball
> and baseball. The school rarely had social affairs.*

Social affairs or not, he had a mythic youth.

My mother said, more than once, "The first time I saw your father I was a little girl—he is years older than I"—she flutters her
old flirt's eyelashes and doesn't specify that he is seven years
older—"and my mother had sent me to the store on a Saturday
afternoon for a loaf of bread. There was a great roar from down
Main Street and a crowd came running, yelling and waving the
Parnassus banners because Parnassus had beat New Kensington
in football, and they were carrying the captain of the football
team on their shoulders and it was your father."

INTERLUDE
The Things My Father Taught Me

THE things my father taught me were these:
How to turn over in bed without disarranging the bedclothes
(you train yourself to lift them slightly and turn under them).

Always to walk on the curb side with a woman, placing her
near to the buildings, otherwise she's "for sale."

Never to "talk shop" at mealtimes, even if it's career people
you're with. (Very hampering this one; talking shop is the point
of New York meals.)

And never relight a cigar you've been smoking and allowed to
go out in an ashtray some time before.

Because he had been an athlete and then a football coach and
a basketball coach, he had a store of vigorous sayings that he
would deliver with a self-mocking grin: "If you don't get a move
on, you're going to get a kick in the slats" (i.e., ribs) or "Try the
horseradish, that'll put lead in your pencil."

A darkened booklet, homemade out of ruled paper—now
turned brown—folded and sewed together (by May?) announces
in Chauncey's handwriting on the cover that:

This Book Contains
Literary Works,
Poems, Idioms, Figures of Speech, and References.

Inside, the booklet has the text of a speech Chauncey made to the Young People's Association of the Parnassus Presbyterian Church on January 25, 1925, the text of a speech he made at a teachers' meeting the first year he taught and was principal at Grinders' Hollow on April 10, 1926, and various quotations from Browning, Mark Twain, Shakespeare, and other reliable sources of wisdom. Most of them are pretty prosy, but one stands out: "There has been more evil wrought in this world by *ignorant* fanatics than by all the *wise* devils."

Chauncey could be a compassionate and thoughtful man. His standards of behavior were as high and constricting as an old-fashioned celluloid collar, however. "I'm tired of looking at that riffraff across the street," he observed once from our screened side porch in Cedar Hill about a perfectly decorous cocktail party the neighbors were having on their lawn.

When I was in college, he said once to me, "You are godly, intelligent, and a gentleman, and that is all that anyone needs to be."

But how very much to have to be.

"TELL ME, MR. KINCAID, ARE YOU A MARRIED MAN?"

LUCILLE and Chauncey were engaged to be married a year before the 1936 flood that devastated the Allegheny valley. They had gone out together for seven or eight years by then.

Chauncey liked Lucille very much, but there were so many other things he wanted to do before he got married.

When he had first gone to college (which his sisters had scrimped and connived for him to do), he had had a professor of Italian who was a very accomplished gentleman. This amazed Chauncey, who was accustomed to "mill-town dagos." Although "Dag" Maglisco had been one of his very best friends in high school, the Magliscos were not what you would call polished.

Things like this showed him that the world was full of a number of things, and a handsome young man, if he minded his manners, might find himself taken up in any number of ways.

After Mr. W. G. Dugan set him up in the Grinders' Hollow School as principal, he continued his own education in summer school. He went to the University of Maine one summer, where he learned to eat lobster. He went to New York University, where he stayed at the Earle Hotel at the corner of Washington

Square. There he made the acquaintance of a permanent guest in the hotel, a dapper older man named Mr. Dargeon. They went to baseball games together, and Mr. Dargeon suggested some Broadway shows they might attend. One night Dargeon walked them up Fifth Avenue a ways, and they went to a French restaurant. Not much of a place, Chauncey thought. The food was all right, although kind of rich and oily; the place certainly didn't look like anything special with just red-checked tablecloths on the tables in a low dark room. But then, when the check came! *Four dollars apiece! Four (1936) dollars!* When you could get a perfectly nice meal at the Freeport Inn at home with white linen tablecloths and napkins and sit on the porch by the river and have roast beef and two kinds of pie for $1.25. Fortunately Chauncey always had enough money in his pocket, so he didn't have to ask for a loan.

Mr. Dargeon noticed that Chauncey paid up without a murmur. A few weeks later when May and Charlotte came over to see him with their friend Maisie McCreight, who drove her car across the mountains and through the new Holland Tunnel, Mr. Dargeon showed them all Chinatown. Then after dinner he took May and Charlotte into Chauncey's room and explained a plan he had, which he had already mentioned to Chauncey. He said that you could invest a certain sum of money each month for two years, and it would bring a tremendous return. He said that he couldn't tell them where their money would be invested because the original owners of the stock had made themselves liable, personally, for any failure and had signed a pledge of secrecy.

Chauncey had been saving money to get married with, but he reasoned that if he made a good bit of money he would be able to get out of teaching and be in all the better position to get married. May said she thought that was wise.

Through the whole next winter Chauncey sent Mr. Dargeon fifty (1936) dollars a month. At last in the spring a brief letter came in pencil from a woman who wrote that her uncle Charles Dargeon had died. Chauncey wrote back asking about the money that had been invested for him, and the woman replied that there was no record of any money having been paid to her uncle in Chauncey's name.

"I always tried to think," said Chauncey, who was a gentleman, after all, "that he intended to invest the money and that he had other calls on it before he could do so."

There was a school board fight at Grinders' Hollow and it became clear to Chauncey that he would have to leave. He was sick of the place anyway; it was just a wide place in the road where education didn't matter as much as the football team. So he went looking.

There was a principalship open at a place called Sligo, up in the high, steely-colored pine woods of northwestern Pennsylvania. The day he went there to be interviewed by the school board was a March day, slashed through by cold rain. He was met at the station, some miles away from the community, which did not even have its own shop on the railroad, by a rangy, furrow-faced farmer wearing an old gray suit and vest but no collar or necktie. The man introduced himself solemnly and led Chauncey to a high old Model T Ford. Chauncey noticed with discouragement there was even a horsedrawn wagon nearby, onto which a man was hoisting sodden sacks of grain.

The school, to his surprise, was a decently built, fairly new red brick building. But when he sat down with the board, his heart sank again. "Do you play cards, Mr. Kincaid?" "Are you regular in your church attendance?" This was more depressing than the ruddy, sweaty boisterousness of the kids he was trying to get away from at Grinders' Hollow. No one said a word about the curriculum, which was very old-fashioned. There was a class in elocution and rhetoric but no languages, not even Latin.

Finally a fat woman with eyes like the heads of steel pins, the only woman on the school board, said to him, "Tell me, Mr. Kincaid, are you a married man?"

Chauncey felt the bile rise in his throat as he smiled and said smoothly, "No, as a matter of fact, I'm not."

"Well," she said, "then we wouldn't be interested in you for this position. We think that a man needs the steadiness and companionship of a Christian marriage in order to lead young people." Her mouth folded in on itself. "And, of course, an unmarried man should not be *exposed* to high school girls on a daily basis."

Chauncey wondered what kind of jezebels the high school girls in Sligo were as he shook the mud of the place from his feet.

By the end of the school term Chauncey had gotten a job teaching English and coaching football in Teaneck, New Jersey. He was excited to be going back to the New York City area, where he had really felt like he was getting somewhere during those years of summer school. Lucille showed that her feelings were hurt by going on dates with the dentist from Greensburg whom her father wanted her to marry.

Chauncey liked Lucille and he let her flutter around him like a butterfly. He followed the line of least resistance, and Lucille's pretty ways amused him. But ever since his mother died when he was a little boy, nobody had been able to pierce the scar that was left. His sisters took easy care of him; before Lucille he had dated the chilly, well-bred Margaret Tourney for several years but one evening, after giving her his customary kiss at the front door, he walked off her front porch and never called her again.

When he first went to Teaneck, he knew he was going to be terribly lonely. He had a desolate feeling of being without anything he knew at all. "I felt like I was encased in a block of ice," he would say in later years.

His first lodging in Teaneck was in a Dutch Colonial house on a shady street owned by a buxom widow with black hair and pink cheeks. The second day he was there, a Sunday, he went down the hall to the bathroom wearing his robe at 9:15 in the morning. The bathroom door was open, and in the crack between the door and the frame he saw the widow standing inside, waiting for him.

He went back to his room, dressed without shaving, packed his suitcase and left, having paid the widow in advance for one week. He felt as humiliated as he had when he was in high school and he had been kissed by a prostitute at a cock fight Ruddy Park had persuaded him to go to. He felt punished for something—he didn't know what—and the disgust he managed finally to summon up was a relief.

The first day of school at lunch one of the teachers said to him, "You're the new teacher from the West, aren't you?" Chauncey replied politely, "I'm new, but I'm not from the West, I'm from Pittsburgh." The woman laughed unpleasantly and said, "That's what I mean; we consider Pittsburgh the West here."

Through two miserable years Chauncey drove back and forth on the Lincoln Highway almost every weekend. At the end of the first year he and Lucille Dinsmore were engaged. At the end of the second year, after the flood and after Quint Dinsmore had lost his job, they were married.

In the fall of that second year, Chauncey had written to Lucille:

My Darling,

I cannot tell you how sad it seems to be going away from you for another year. For the first time I don't mind it, strangely enough, although I shall miss you more than I would miss the sun. But now, you see, I feel that I belong to someone—at last. So, although I miss hearing your voice and seeing your lovely eyes and hearing you laugh, I know that I am in your heart and mind's eye, so I don't mind.

> *With all my love, forever,*
> *Chauncey*

THE HAT

"MAY never wanted Chauncey to get married," said my mother. "She was all sweet and everything, but somehow there were always obstacles."

Her fine old hands, "lady's hands" as she boasted, held a cigarette in the winter afternoon gloom of her small Pittsburgh living room; the smoke curled through the dusk like mist.

My father was well into his thirties before he married my mother. "Things were very confused there for a while," said Mother. "Daddy—Grandpa—had lost his job—it was the Depression—and he and Ruby had gone to the Farm and I was living at Aunt Hallie's where they didn't really want me very much, and, oh I don't know, it was just a mess."

Stories, it was always stories when I came from New York to pay a weekend duty visit, so compulsory in its summoning up of feelings, so much less satisfactory than a leisurely phone call that occasionally blossomed into conversation, grandly disregarding the AT&T long-distance rates. (We were prodigal with living expenses; Western Pennsylvania is Upper Appalachia, and my family had a Southern disregard for domestic economies. "We never had any money but we ate well," my mother would say.)

This time there was a new story in Mother's repertoire. In my parents' modest section of smart, pushy Cedar Hill, where they had now lived for thirty-five years, a neighbor two nights before had slashed her wrists and then cut her own throat.

My parents had hardly known the woman, although she was their contemporary, seventy-five or so. Isolated in their hermetic winter dressing of storm windows, furled awnings, and early darkness, the miniature Tudor, Colonial, and Cape Cod houses on the street might each have been sitting on the grand acreage of their full-size prototypes instead of lined up like cereal boxes on a shelf. "This is city living," Mother said, jangling her bracelets, "I never see anyone from one day's end to the next."

But somehow she knew (a neighbor was getting his car out for an early morning trip to the airport when the medics arrived . . . she was at the bank when the lawyer came in . . .) that Dotty Ross had died. "She was a sweet woman," my mother said when I arrived for my quarterly visit, rushing in irrationally angry at the peripatetic tedium of cab to La Guardia, waiting in the lounge, plane to Pittsburgh, cab to Daffodil Lane, where my mother sat smoking and my father sat in his big platform rocker watching the last of the season's football games on television.

"The son çame home but the daughter didn't," said Mother.

Once, when I was about ten years old, thirty years ago, I had gone there to play with that little boy and I remembered his mother standing in a long, pale green corridor, as slender and silently radiant as a candle.

"But what could have made her do it?"

"She was never happy," said Mother. "She was a Catholic, you know, and he was Jewish."

The old Pittsburgh categorizations. Presbyterian nice people, the black people who worked for them, and then Jews, with Catholics out "beyond God's knowledge" as one of my great-aunts used to say.

"You know, for them," said my mother, "that's a sin"—the Catholics, she meant, and suicide—"but"—Mother held her cigarette away from her mouth, which trembled—"surely God will forgive her."

We then returned safely, as we always did, to the more distant past, the one that lay secure in the illuminated pages of Mother's memory. With the great bloody fact of Mrs. Ross's suicide filling the moment, we could only return in our talk to Parnassus and the old stories.

We went to lunch at a fast-food restaurant where the psychedelic green of the plastic parsley lining the serving trays complemented the lettuce in the salad bar (Stouffer's, where they had lunched in the English Room for the first fifteen years of their retirement with an old-maid Latin teacher and a widowed algebra teacher, had closed), and then I sat in the kitchen while my mother played solitaire and smoked—and talked about the past, her past, of course.

That was when, the calamitous end of Mrs. Ross's marriage weighing on her mind, my mother said, "May never wanted your father to get married."

"Why not?"

"Well, she liked having a man around. Otherwise she was just left with Charlotte, and you know what that was like."

The two old-maid aunts, May and Charlotte, resented their mutual dependence as the roof and timbers of an old country barn, creaking and groaning, resent their mutual shelter and support.

"When I was a senior in high school," she said, "our French teacher took us to hear a play put on in French by some Belgian glassworkers down the Monongahela River, and your father was the French teacher's date. I thought he was pretty cute, and he thought I was pretty cute, but, of course, we couldn't do anything about it *then*."

Some years later, when Lucille had graduated from teachers' college, Chauncey had asked her out. They went to Pittsburgh to see a traveling road company matinee of *No, No, Nanette* and afterward had dinner in the Winter Garden at the William Penn Hotel. It was heady stuff, and she began to like him even more.

He would send strapping senior boys—the sons of Polish miners—in from his country school to take her out to him when he had to stay late to chaperon a dance ("You know, when those boys are eighteen, they're *men*," Mother would say); she bought him a set of mother-of-pearl evening studs and cuff links to wear with a rented dinner jacket for the Junior Women's Club dance, "Le Bal Moderne."

They took her cousin Jane Hamilton and Chauncey's friend Ruddy Park to football games at Washington and Jefferson College in "Little Washington," Pennsylvania, where Chauncey had gone to school, and once Jane left her fox furs in the car and they were stolen.

It was the stuff of memory and myth. "I was very happy," said Lucille, "but, of course, I went out with other people too."

One of the other people was Paul Fleming, the preacher's son. He was handsome ("not as handsome as your father") and very debonair, and he went to Carnegie Tech to school and then he married, so that was the end of that. ("Some Society girl from Pittsburgh got her hooks into him.")

And then Chauncey decided to go to New York University summer school to get his master's degree, and that was when the trouble started.

"Chauncey thought that he could get more money and a better chance of advancement if he had a master's degree, and May, in her quiet way, encouraged him in that," said Lucille. "They were great for education, you know, the Kincaids. Well, then, when he had registered and signed up and was going to be away all summer in New York, come to find out that, of course, he couldn't afford to get married too.

"So that went on for three summers, and then, when he had his degree, and went to the school board out there in Grinders' Hollow to ask for more money, well, they said they didn't have it and he had too many degrees for them, so perhaps he'd better look someplace else.

"So then he had the bee in his bonnet that he'd like to go over East to New York, since he'd enjoyed summer school so much. And May encouraged him in *that*.

"So he taught for two years in Teaneck, New Jersey. And right around that time was when Daddy, my father, lost his job, and I had to go to Aunt Hallie's to live.

"Chauncey always thought my father was spoiled and just did what he wanted—well, of course, Chauncey is a little bit like that himself—so we had arguments and twice I gave Chauncey back his ring, and once I told him I never wanted to see him again. Only I had left my evening slippers in his car, so he called the next day and said, 'I know you never want to see me again, but perhaps you'd at least like your shoes back?' "

She laughed. "It would have been like me to have done that deliberately, but really I hadn't.

"In any case, by then I think May encouraged him in his fear that if we got married, he'd have to support my parents, so that went on for a year or two. Finally, there was a dentist from Vandergrift who really wanted to marry me, so I gave Chauncey back his ring and told him I was going to marry the dentist from Vandergrift. Well, that did it, more or less, and we were married at last.

"But I never quite trusted May.

"When we were first married we lived in one of the nice apartments above the Kroger Grocery Store, across the railroad tracks and the park from Aunt Hallie. It all just looked darling. I had a sectional davenport which was the latest thing and yellow dining room chairs in the provincial style with flowers painted on them. But we did have to help Daddy and Ruby. I was teaching and I did it out of my money. I never asked Chauncey for a penny.

"Well, one year just before Easter, May called and said she had seen a hat from Horne's advertised in the paper, and she thought it would be just right for me."

My mother loved hats and could inventory when she had bought each cloche and garden-party hat and off-the-face and Empress Eugenie and Robin-Hood-with-a-feather and 1950s clip (like an enlarged barrette) and early 1960s bouffant shape covered in silk flowers and on through the general demise of hats in the seventies and eighties. She still indefatigably appeared in spring hats in February and fall hats in August, so as to be the first that season. Furthermore, she tagged specific events by the hat she wore: "When we heard about Pearl Harbor we were on our way to May and Charlotte's for Sunday evening supper, and I had just put on a new hat trimmed with monkey fur. It was very beautiful."

"Anyway, May, of course ordered all of Charlotte's clothes for her. She'd point out things in the paper and Charlotte would say yea and nay (yea if she knew what was good for her), and May would have them sent out on approval. So May told me there was this hat and should she order it on her charge and I could pay her?

"The hat was thirty dollars. That was in 1942 and May knew that I no more had thirty dollars for a hat than the man in the moon, but she kept insisting and wanted to send for it and saying that if I didn't like it, we could send it back."

"What was it like?" I asked.

"I don't remember," she said with disdain.

"Now I had said once to Chauncey that I intended to help my father and Ruby, and I never said anything more about it. When we deposited our checks I took a certain amount out of mine each month, which we understood was for general expenses: groceries and Colored Hallie to clean and so forth. Chauncey took the rent and payments for the car and other things out of his. I paid my father out of mine, but I had never said anything about it, except that once, to Chauncey. I didn't think it would be nice"—a word freighted with moral consequence to my mother—"not to tell him I was helping Daddy, but it upset him so I never said anything more, and I never told him how much.

"He used to talk from time to time to May—just a sentence here and there, you know. They just lived two blocks away, and we didn't get the morning paper and they did, so Chauncey would go over there to pick it up. It was funny; May aggravated him by being so bossy, but she was the one he talked to, not Charlotte.

"I think he talked to them about things he didn't talk to me about. In a way, of course, he was their little boy, but I don't know, when married people don't talk. . . ."

The specter of Mrs. Ross and her suicide drifted across both of our minds like illicit smoke in a movie theater intrusively hovering in front of the story on the screen.

"In any case, May insisted that time about the hat, and I just kept saying no until she finally let it drop."

"How much were you sending your father?"

"Thirty dollars a month."

A BIGGER WORLD

Said the little red rooster to the little red hen,
"You haven't laid an egg since the Lord knows when."
Said the little red hen to the little red rooster,
"Well, you don't come around as often as you use-ter."

THERE were, in those schools where Ruby and Lucille and Chauncey and Charlotte and May's friends taught, old teachers who had come in from the country and who sat, wrinkled and wry, behind desks where the chalky smell of the blackboard met and clashed with the fresh, grassy smell of the children day after day. The teachers passed judgment on each other—"She was strict but she was fair"; "She couldn't teach a cat how to drink milk"—and were blasé and tender in turn with the children. They gave up their lives year after year, preparing people to leave them. "The rule of three" that appeared in the handwritten arithmetic book with the date 1794 in a chest at the Farm was replaced with *McGuffey's Reader* and the blue-backed speller; after World War I classes in hygiene and French fancified the curriculum; after World War II Dick and Jane and Baby Sally spouted their everlasting imperative to "See Spot run." Then ethnic consciousness was institutionalized and the standards that Georg Lutvig in his copybook had struggled to meet with his rule of three were found to be only relative. "The King's English" was found to be only a dialect after all, but still the teachers cajoled and demanded and led logically from step to step; still they said "Boys and girls!"; still some commanded by force and some by personality and some not at all. There were among them inquiring minds and inventive minds and for some it was just a job; they weren't the guardians of culture, they weren't the makers of democracy, but still, when all was said and done, there had been something given by the teachers. Chauncey remembered Ruskin's dicta on art all his life; Lucille pointed out palmate and pinnate leaves on a walk in the woods when Quint took me up the lane above the springhouse at the Farm . . . scraps of French, scraps of astronomy, the Big Dipper in the night sky—it was a bigger world those old teachers held the key to.

In Georg Lutvig's 1794 copybook, on a page of doodling there is part of a geography lesson:

Dundee a considerable town in Scotland . . .
Denmark one of the northern Kingdoms of Europe
Corsica an island . . .
Catherine Bolinger hir hand and pen

When Lucille taught second grade in 1930, some of the old teachers working with her had started in one-room country schools. While those teachers grew older, their hopes and dreams became impersonal, eternal, embodied in those forever young children coming through the door each fall. They aged in their impersonality but did not seem to intimate mortality in that aging; they aged but they were permanent—as permanent and as potential as the Gilbert Stuart portrait of Washington that hung forever unfinished above the first-grade blackboard.

*   *   *

My mother often referred to the children in her second-grade classes as "the littles." She found them to be infinitely lovable but prone to wickedness and error. She was strict and nothing escaped her, but that meant the needy as well as the bad. If a little boy had been struggling with his reading lesson all morning without much success, he would likely be given a gold star and his name written on the blackboard for having helped to pass out the songbooks; if a little girl was fat and perhaps a bit messy, Lucille would compliment her in front of the class on her pretty curls.

She was very loving to her little people, hugging and kissing them a lot, and, as the best teachers do, she treated them as equals in a way. She did not talk down to them. "Robert and I are puzzled about why that cherry tree in the school yard is so late in blooming," she would say, she and Robert being together in their puzzlement. She also, of course, when telling about things later, adored making jokes about how she had protected her superiority by pretending to know things she did not. She could be cruel if the children did not do what she wanted them to—such as putting tape across their mouths when they talked without permission. She was complicated, like all people, and not above changing her tune when it suited her.

When I was a young man spending some time in Paris on an extended tour just after college, I was sitting in the Luxembourg Gardens one silvery green spring day. Nearby the little boys from a private-school class were playing vigorously around the urbane trunks of some shaped plane trees. Two teachers, an older woman wearing a brown coat and a plain young woman in a gray coat with a knitted gray hat pulled down over her ears, were chatting animatedly. "*Oh, mais oui,*" the younger woman said and shrugged, and then, suddenly, one little boy tussling with another one took his friend's head in both hands and began to bang it hard against the tree trunk. Both teachers looked over, and the younger took one slouching step across to the boys, pulled them apart, and said, "*Doucement! Doucement!*" She gave a Gallic shrug and continued her conversation with her colleague without further ado. Teachers take it all in stride.

As the years went by, Lucille felt herself coming closer and closer to the state of withered wisdom of the old maids she taught with. She took drama classes at Carnegie Tech (she had always wanted to be an actress; in her high school yearbook when everybody else wrote something funny as their life's ambition, she simply wrote the word *actress*), but when she proposed taking a year off and registering in a drama school in Boston, her father said, "Oh, don't do it this year, wait a year and then if you still want to, I'll support you." She knew she wouldn't do what he didn't want.

And Chauncey Kincaid kept going to school in distant places and changing jobs and not quite committing himself to getting married. Lucille didn't want to become an eccentric old maid; there were too many eccentrics around who made the best of tattered lives. She wanted someone for herself. She knew, when she looked at the perfect little ears of little boys in her class, the rosebud mouths of little girls, their impishness, and their dependence on her, that she wanted a baby.

When Lucille and Chauncey finally got married in 1939 ("Give me a kiss, old pal o' mine, this is Christmas 1939," Lucille would sing for the rest of her life), and they moved into one of the apartments in the Kroger Grocery Store building on Fourth Street in Parnassus, Lucille was completely happy. She loved her apartment and she loved Chauncey.

Each of them was securely the apple of someone's eye for the first time since they were children, and they played like children—or like newlyweds. He called her "Joe" because there was a little Italian boy across the hall named Joe, and in some complicated private joke the name got transferred to Lucille. (To the end of his long, long life he would call her that, so that in the nursing home where they both were finally trapped he was thought to be disoriented because one day, feeling dizzy in the hall, he called for "Joe"—the one person he trusted.) They laughed a lot; he doubled up over the time she called out the window as he left to do errands, "Bring home a loaf of bread from the store," and a little street kid ran after him and said, "Mister, your mother wants you to bring home a loaf of bread." She would dance up to him in the living room with its two platform rockers or in the bedroom with its bird's-eye maple suite, her delicate fists doubled, and say, "You wanta fight? You wanta fight, buster?" and he, after a couple of feints, would pull her to his warm, massive chest.

They were happy for a time.

After a while, though, the soap bubble of their world burst without their even noticing it. Chauncey got older—he had turned forty less than a year after they were married—and his black spells would come on him when, as he once wrote to her from Teaneck, everything seemed "hard, hopeless, and gloomy." World War II erupted and played out its apocalypse with distant thunder around the world. Chauncey and Lucille spent Saturday afternoons scanning the skies as enemy aircraft watchers in a tower out in the countryside near Congruity, and the futility of the gesture seemed to Lucille like an image of the futility of her life. She wanted a baby.

Chauncey did not.

He made out elaborate budgets for them on big sheets of yellow graph paper, and he took everything into account, so to speak: church money (ten percent of their combined teachers' salaries after taxes—"I can't help what the government takes," said Lucille), money for his cigars, money to go to the movies, and money for the old washwoman out in West's Hollow, as well as the necessities of rent and food and clothes. He pointed out patiently why there was no money for a child. Lucille thought of his story about crying when he was a little boy because his mother was dead and his father had left home and there was no money for any dinner except roly-poly pudding without any meat or vegetables to go with it and she held her peace.

After two or three years of marriage, at Christmastime Lucille again broached the subject of having a child with Chauncey. "Well, you'll have to quit teaching if you have a baby and then, if something would happen to me, you'd be stuck with a baby and no time to earn your living." He had paused and said in a tight, contained voice, "And with your father out of work and him and Ruby living at the Farm, I don't think you want to get stuck out there." Chauncey did not have much respect for Quint as a breadwinner, and it was typical of Chauncey to leap ahead to the worst possibility and typical that for him Quint was the worst possibility.

Lucille didn't say anything more, but a few weeks later she slipped on the ice and pulled some tendons in her leg. She had to use crutches, and as the drab, raw month of March dragged itself into spring, she didn't get any better. She didn't let the crutches slow her down. Once May, who worked across the railroad tracks from the Kroger apartments in the Keystone Dairy office, looked out of her window and saw Lucille climbing up the fire-escape stairs on her crutches carrying a bag of groceries and a pot of flowering geraniums. The next thing Lucille knew, a low, vibrant, male voice said very gently behind her, "Don't be frightened. I'm right behind you, and I'm going to reach around and take the bag and the flowers from you, so just be still." It was Jack Love, whom May had sent over from the dairy office to head off the sure catastrophe on the stairs. All told, Lucille used the crutches for twenty-two weeks, as she would proudly recount— more than five months—but Chauncey was not persuaded that it would make her feel better to have a baby. Not that time.

Lucille had never called Naomi Vogel again after Naomi failed to show up for the surprise engagement party Lucille had given for her. Nor had Naomi called her. When they passed each other on the street, they nodded and said hello as people do in a small town, but that was all. But then a couple of years after she had used the crutches for twenty-two weeks, Lucille heard that Naomi (who had, of course, married Luther Russell) was expecting a baby. This time Lucille set to work in earnest. She moved herself and Chauncey into a house on Monticello Hill owned by her Aunt Myra, who did not charge her a high rent. There were two spare bedrooms. Lucille's allergies, which had first manifested themselves when her father married Ruby, returned, and with them her vulnerabilities. "I was so unhappy because I felt bad all the time," she would say. "And every day when Chauncey came home from teaching down at Cedar Hill (he didn't get home until an hour or so after I did), I would just burst into tears when I saw him. Every day I would think, 'I'm *not* going to do that,' but I just couldn't help it."

And then, around Christmastime again, after Christmas Day dinner at the Farm and a second Christmas night dinner with May and Charlotte, Lucille and Chauncey got on the night train for New York, where they spent four days going to shows and having a fine time.

And I was born nine months later.

The morning I was born, my father, bounding down the steps of the Citizens' General Hospital with his hat three sizes bigger and beaming on all the world, ran into Naomi Russell on the sidewalk. "How's Lucille?" she asked, knowing, as people do in a small town, that my mother was in the hospital. "She just had a fine baby boy—with red hair," my father exulted. "I'm *glad*," said Naomi warmly.

When my mother left the hospital with me she couldn't go home right away because there had been some confusion about having the smallest bedroom painted and things weren't quite ready. She couldn't go out to the Farm because it was August, and the only spare room was up under the roof and as hot as a flickers' nest. So she and Chauncey and the baby spent a few days at Charlotte and May's. The first morning, when Lucille had gotten up early with the baby, she knocked on May's door and said, laughingly, "Do you want a man in your bed?" And so that is where I was put.

Part Four

GETTING
AWAY

INTERLUDE

A FTER Chauncey and Lucille were married and I was born, life took on the pleasant monotony of a well-known game, with only a little room for chance. Sunday was church and then dinner at Charlotte and May's ("We were *invited* every Sunday," said my mother), every other Friday night was bridge club, there were trips to the Farm and dinner—often just my mother and me; my father kept the same slightly contemptuous civility toward Quint he had always had—and in the summer, when school was out, we went away.

I had friends—the little Ommaneys two doors down, Melissa Steiner across the street ("a mean child if ever there were one"), Bobby Shearer-who-had-a-bicycle. But the important people were grown-ups and the important grown-ups came in pairs: Mother and Daddy, Grandpa and Grandma, Aunt Charlotte and Aunt May. The Stewart great-aunts, who came singly, were odd, eccentric, difficult; they could have the effect of a sudden thunderstorm, dampening plans and sending people scurrying, but there was no staying power.

THE ANAGRAM

WHEN I was about ten years old my mother would occasionally get phone calls during which she would be very cold and barely polite and then, when she hung up, snarl, "That trashy woman with her 'Myrie' this and 'Myrie' that—all she wants is Aunt Myra's money. Oh, I can't stand her." This was so unusual for my mother, who seemed at least to like everyone, that I always asked who the woman was. Mother invariably answered, "It's that Bill Lochran's wife."

Aunt Myra, a great-aunt, a Stewart, a sister of rich Aunt Hallie and of my dead grandmother Jean, was a grand, grim old woman with blue hair and a set of dentures that gave her the jaw of George Washington. Unlike the two old-maid Kincaid aunts who were part of the daily round, Aunt Charlotte chattering and Aunt May conniving into our lives all the time, Aunt Myra had the place of a family portrait. She impressed with the majesty of her image and connections to the past, but, except by my mother whom she coddled, Aunt Myra was not taken very seriously by anyone.

She lived alone in a cluttered, rather bleak house, which she had shared with her late husband, a second cousin much older than she named Alonzo Anderson Alter. A sometime newspaperman, Uncle Lon had spent a year at Harvard in his youth, coming out of the backwoods of Western Pennsylvania, and apparently was never able to settle down after that to an extended period of work for gain. Asked once by sharp-tongued Aunt Hallie why Lon didn't look for a job, Aunt Myra had replied that it would hurt his pride. To which Aunt Hallie replied that *she* was thankful *her* husband didn't have any fancy degrees—he just supported his family.

Aunt Myra spent her time as the matron of the local Eastern Star chapter and in pursuing dusty research into DAR credentials among various ancestors. Her dining room table, piled high with ledgers and newspapers, sometimes held a little pile of letters on creamy, spotted parchment, looking as though they had been delivered out of a time machine, so conspicuously ancient were they. Reproached for the state of her house by Aunt Hallie, Aunt Myra replied, "I have a soul above a broom."

Aunt Myra had taught school, like almost everyone else in our family, but she had taught in a vocational high school in one of the tough districts of Pittsburgh because the pay was best there. I knew that there was a student whom she had tried to help after school hours and whom she had kept up with in later life—"a talented young man who wanted to better himself," she is supposed to have said. "A pretty-boy con man," my mother called him. Visiting him after he was married, she had fallen on the ice, breaking a hip, and ever after that she was a figure in a wheelchair, hunched and impassive as the Rock of Ages.

It was after this that the wife of Bill Lochran, Aunt Myra's protégé, would call my mother to find out how "Myrie" was.

That was all I knew for a number of years until one June when I had just graduated from high school and I went up to Parnassus to spend a few days with, first, my grandparents in the country and then Aunt Charlotte and Aunt May in town. Parnassus, when I came in to the aunts', was in its kindly spring mood. The leaves on the heavy old trees meeting across the brick streets were just in full leaf, but the light was still pale, not summer hard, and the shabby wooden houses looked to be soft-edged rather than in need of a paint job.

The first evening we had chicken baked in cream sauce with onions and new potatoes and fresh asparagus. After dinner Aunt May did the dishes and Aunt Charlotte worked on figures in the church account books. I lounged around, browsing through a stack of old *Saturday Evening Posts*.

The next afternoon I walked up to Monticello Hill, where Aunt Myra lived, climbing the worn cement steps, which mounted the bluff behind old Parnassus, shortcutting the switch-back road angling across the cliff face. At the top, the streets laid out after World War I, Argonne, where my mother and Quint and Ruby had once lived, and Pershing, sagged around the top of the hill in concentric circles. Rows of 1920s bungalows, tired as banners hanging in the VFW hall, were interspersed with Cape Cod cottages in brick. I had worn shorts and the wind whipping through my legs was cool, although the sun in those streets, still nearly treeless after forty years, was hot. Aunt Myra lived in a larger, older house on the street farthest back by Farm Hill, one of the first houses in all the Monticello Division. Inside, the light coming through net curtains was dust-filled and yellow as the pile of letters on the corner of the dining room table.

As it had become harder and harder for her to get out of her wheelchair, Aunt Myra had had to take on some help. Oddly for someone so austere in appearance, she had a completely emo-tional relationship with whomever worked for her, imposing pointless demands, nursing hurt feelings, refusing help when it was most necessary. Finally she had been reduced to a retarded woman with crossed eyes who wore a bibbed apron and was, said Ruby, putting the cap on it, "a Free Methodist," naming a rabid sect next door, we thought, to the Holy Rollers. The woman, jabbering like a monkey at whoever got within her ken, scared the bejesus out of me, but I had come for a visit and visit I would.

After I was seated on the plush couch, which scratched my bare legs, Aunt Myra asked me to bring her some of the old let-ters. The packet was tied with a brown grosgrain ribbon. She slowly untied the ribbon, drawing it out of the bow as though she were stroking something. "These letters were written to my great-grandfather, Samuel Stewart," she said. "They came from his aunt, Mary Stewart, in Killinchy, Ireland. I don't know what should be done with them when I'm gone." She sniffed and pulled a handkerchief out of her voile bosom.

The top letter was addressed in a pale brown ink to:

Samuel Stewart
the son of James Stewart
near Pine Roon
Simon Drum Post Office
Greensburg State of Pennsylvania
America

Just then there was a sound of a door opening in the kitchen and Mrs. Evans's jabbering. Aunt Myra did not turn her head as a tall man with dark hair wearing a grubby, light-colored windbreaker appeared in the dining room doorway. He had prominent cheekbones, scarred skin, and deep-set light eyes; his trousers, part of an old suit, were baggy and, like the jacket and the scarred skin, set off his good looks by contrast.

"Mister, she fall, she don't do what I tell her, then she fall, she don't let me do what I do for her like a good Christian, I'm a Christian woman, I don't take no backseat, I'm a Christian woman—" Mrs. Evans trailed him to the living room.

"Myra, how are you?" Bill Lochran's voice was warm. (There was no question that it was he—the deserving former student or the con man, depending on who was telling the tale.) You immediately trusted this man.

Aunt Myra just shook her head up and down to his question, not committing herself to her condition. "This is my nephew," she said, indicating me.

Bill Lochran nodded at me and grinned; he put his hand on Aunt Myra's shoulder and Mrs. Evans, with a couple more mutters of "I'm a Christian woman. . . ." subsided to the kitchen, spluttering.

"How are the girls?" asked Aunt Myra.

"They're okay." Bill Lochran sat down with his knees spread wide apart and his elbows resting on them. His hands, dangling down between his knees, were big and white with jagged nails sunk in grease stains. "Nice day, huh?" It wasn't particularly, but it didn't matter. He grinned again, enfolding Aunt Myra and me in complicity.

"Would you hand me my purse, William?" Aunt Myra indicated her black purse with a green glass clasp sitting on a jumbled table nearby. "I have asked Mrs. Evans time and again to leave it within my reach, but she simply doesn't hear me." The Stewarts all put on airs in their speech; Aunt Hallie customarily said "don-cha know" and used a mock Irish accent like grand dowagers in the movies. Most of us would have said "Mrs. Evans doesn't *listen* to me," and I was impressed.

"Doesn't shut up long enough to hear." Bill Lochran shook his head. "She spits, too." Resentfully he brushed a heavy hand down the lapel of his jacket toward the pocket, which he reached into and pulled a pack of Camels from. He shook one out, tapped it on the pack, and lit it with one hand in a virtuoso display.

He looked at Aunt Myra's purse but seemed reluctant to associate himself too eagerly with it.

I looked at it.

Mrs. Evans, perking like a teakettle, shot into the dining room from the kitchen and yelled, "Your lunch is here, there's lunch, I put food for everybody on the table 'cause I'm a Christian woman, and I don't believe in goin' without when there's food." She stumped toward Aunt Myra and already had her hands on the handles of the wheelchair when Aunt Myra said, "William, I have a bad hand now. You will have to feed me."

"Okay, sure." He stood up and smiled again so that everything was just fine.

Mrs. Evans shoved Aunt Myra's wheelchair toward the dining room and whirled her around to a place at the head of the table. There were three places set, and Aunt Myra, pulling herself together, said coldly to Mrs. Evans, "Mr. Lochran and my nephew are here to take care of me. You can eat in the kitchen."

Mrs. Evans was so startled that, with one mutter about being a Christian woman, she took off.

Behind Aunt Myra there was a round-fronted china closet with dusty glass, and above it there was an ancient oval photograph in a gilt and dark wood frame. It was a portrait of a woman wearing a white frilled cap and it had faded so that there was nothing visible of the face except two dark, deep-set, penetrating eyes and a strong jawline. Aunt Myra opened her mouth, moving that same jaw as the woman in the portrait, and Bill Lochran spooned in franks and beans. He did it kindly but he had never taken off his jacket and he didn't linger over the process, while she stretched her massive head with its crown of blue hair almost languorously toward him.

I felt that I was part of a natural disaster. In thinking about it much later, I believe that what upset me was not only the reversal of order and revelation of physical need (which embarrasses any young person in an older person), but the fact that I was indeed witnessing an act of private communion. As with the much more powerful, vital Aunt May down on Fifth Avenue whose relationship with her old boss Mr. Love was carried on in late-night phone calls and his pseudo-clandestine visits to deliver the evening paper, so here, as Bill Lochran fed Aunt Myra her lunch, there occurred something possible only for the two people doing it. I was a very orderly young man and I had no category for what I saw.

Lunch seemed to last as long as a toothache, but at last it was over. Aunt Myra said to me, "Now William and I have to conduct some business, and I know your aunts downtown will be anxious about you." This was sarcastic; she was terribly jealous of the other aunts.

I fled.

All that afternoon I was in a deep depression. I mooned around Aunt May's house, lounging on the glider in the shade of the front porch, pretending to read *Return of the Native*, which I had brought with me, but the torrents of feeling and broken weirs and vast heaths in that book were like demon fingers plucking on my jangled nerves.

Aunt Charlotte bustled about inside, and at last Aunt May came home after the odd lacuna in her day between noontime leaving of the Buick agency where she kept the books in her semiretirement and three-thirty, when she appeared on her own front steps. Jack Love's house was in the next block of Fifth Avenue, between "upstreet" and home, but nobody ever asked where she had been for those three hours.

Maisie McCreight, the horse-faced old maid whose voice would shatter glass—a useful attribute for her career as a sixth-grade teacher—was coming for dinner and going to stay afterward as a fourth so that I could get on with my bridge. Just before dinner, when Maisie McCreight and I were sitting in the living room while Aunt Charlotte put the water glasses on the table, the doorbell rang.

Aunt May passed by the door to the front hall. I heard her voice briefly, and then she appeared in the living room doorway. "There's a nice little country girl selling strawberries here," she said to me, "will you go and choose some for dessert." Aunt May never condescended to explain. She moved back to the kitchen like a ship sailing into port, and I dragged myself to the doorway. The girl was too plump and wearing shorts that were too short. She had frizzy red hair and very white skin; a small pimple glowed sorely at the corner of her mouth. I said, "Hi," and glowered at the strawberries. She said, "You want some?" I chose two boxes and paid her from the money on the marble-topped hall table.

When I returned to the living room, Aunt May was talking to Maisie. "Wasn't she a pretty little girl?" she asked me with a slow smile.

I felt like I had been hit with a cannonball. Before dinner Aunt May had asked if I were going to change out of my shorts into trousers, with a speculative look at my long young legs. I had said no then; it was only Maisie coming for dinner and it was summer.

Now I shouted, "I'm going upstairs to change my shorts." At the door I choked out, "She was horrible."

Both aunts and Maisie looked as though the print of Blue Boy over the piano had suddenly spoken up. Aunt Charlotte, in the dining room doorway with water pitcher atilt, asked helplessly, "What's wrong with the lad?"

The summer went by and then fall came. I went off to college to be given all of Western Civilization with which to classify those feelings I had no place for. Aunt Myra, in her grand historic dereliction up on the hill, careened from catastrophe to disaster, Mrs. Evans capering in attendance. Finally her bad leg was amputated and by the next spring she was dead.

Ruby and sharp, raddled Aunt Hallie cleaned out her house, throwing out bags and bags of electric bills, DAR committee reports, and bank statements. They had lived in that town for decades, in those families that served as ministers of the past, so while professing a disdain for the old days (" 'Twas the rest of the family wanted to spend their time digging up the dead, not I," said Aunt Hallie), they saved, as carefully as any curators, pieces of monumental mahogany, tortured by the jigsaw, and old photographs, including the lady over the china closet, and bundles of letters from—as Aunt Hallie said—"before Noah's flood."

They came eventually to me, those artifacts, and in another summer I put together the outlines and shapes of lives, shadowy but gripping as the eyes of the lady in the portrait. I found the bundle of letters tied with the cinnamon-colored ribbon Aunt Myra had toyed with, teasing me into attention, the day I had met Bill Lochran. The letters were from an old lady in Ireland in the 1820s to her American nephew, Captain Samuel Stewart, and concerned the unsuccessful visit of his cousin, also named Samuel. Cousin Samuel had gone to Ireland because Aunt Mary Stewart wanted an heir.

This is what the letters said:
Aunt Mary, left alone after her parents died near the village of

Killinchy in Northern Ireland, her two brothers, James and John, having emigrated to Pennsylvania in the 1770s, wrote neatly to ask something very specific. She wanted company. There was an unmarried son of her brother John, a favorite and spoiled son himself about whom his old father complained in letters written a generation before "Never thanks it worth his Wheel to truble to Wrate to me," who she thought might be the one to come.

Aunt Mary spoke in a clear, decisive voice, though given to pious reflection, as old ladies may be. She had a slight Irish accent in her letters: Cousin Samuel, her chosen one, will be "doubly *Dar* to me"; Captain Samuel in America lives on "Pine *Roon*," not Pine Run; and, bitten with the promise of the New World, even Aunt Mary wondered whether she might "leave *me* native country."

The accent was to echo down in the grand talk of the Stewarts. Aunt Hallie laughed about her grandmother, who disparaged the "darety, feelthy, shanty Irish" (meaning the Catholics) in an accent so thick you could cut it with a knife. But Aunt Hallie herself, born out at Markle on Pine Run, pronounced "were" as "ware" until the day she died.

Aunt Mary's Irish voice promising the inheritance of her lease lured Cousin Samuel across the waters on a journey of miles and months. He arrived in the village of Killinchy on the third of July, 1823, and Aunt Mary wrote to Captain Samuel, "I may truly say that I was glad to see him on the account that he was the son of such a near relation and I being so Destitute of Friends in this Country. . . ."

But Cousin Samuel was a new man, an American, accustomed to life in the wooded round hills of Pennsylvania where thirty years before the farmers had been the center of the insurrection against the new United States federal government and its hated tax on whiskey.

Such a man as Samuel Stewart could use dissatisfaction with the government as a peg to hang any personal discontent on. So Aunt Mary, after saying that her loneliness and Samuel's being the son of a favorite brother combined to make "his arrival here doubly Dar to me," goes on to tell that "in a short time I was sorry to learn that he was not pleased with this Country":

I Believe the Climate made no unfavorable alternation either on his health or Constitution; Yet he seems to think our method of living in this Country so very far Inferior to that in America that he is daily longing to be home again; and Rent tithe Cefs [?] and other taxes seems to him such systems of Oppreason that he can never think of allowing the fruits of his Industry to be laid on in that way—

She says impartially that

I must acknowledge that you enjoy many advantages in America that we have not here Yet when we compair our markets to yours and the many conveniences we have resulting from them that our situation is not so bad as it might appear at first sight. Land is so well in this country that although the farms is small ther is great Quantity brought to market and the [illegible] is good and enables Farmer [illegible] to meet all [illegible].

Aunt Mary recounts the prices she gets for her crops:

Wheat sells this season at 16s . . . 0 pence . . . 112 pound
Oats . . . . 10 . . . . 0 p . . . . . . Bsl
Pork . . . . 2.5 . . . 6 p . . . . . . 120 pound
Butter . . . . 0.0 . . 10 p . . . . . . Pound
Beef . . . . 1.10 . . . . 0 to 2 Pounds
P 120
And all other articles in Proporation for ready money.

Ireland had an urban population large enough to provide good markets for perishable items such as pork and beef and butter. Western Pennsylvania, still largely a rural community, had no place to dispose of such items, and only grains and vegetables or secondary products such as wool, linen, and whiskey could be transported and sold. A Pittsburgh bookseller, Zadok Cramer, who annually published an almanac and a guide to the rivers called *The Navigator*, noted in 1808 that the Monongahela region produced wheat, rye, barley, oats, buckwheat, corn, and potatoes "in great abundance," Monongahela flour brought the highest price of any flour in the market at New Orleans, and "the best and greatest quantity of rye whiskey is made on this river."

No Pennsylvania farm, however, bursting with promise as it may have been, could compare with the security of Ireland for Aunt Mary:

> *I had some idea of Going to Ammerica But Now upon a*
> *second Consideration finds that it would not answer me to leave*
> *me native Country. I am now Pretty far advanced in Years*
> *and was I to go to Ammerica and Loose my health at my time*
> *of Life I might become a burthen to my friends and a*
> *trouble to myself. . . .*

Cousin Samuel, she had thought, would be just the ticket. So he spent from July of 1823 until sometime in 1825 in Ireland, where he proved to be unhappy with more than rents, tithes, and taxes. He managed to find reasons outside himself for his troubles. The American notion of the free man gave him the excuse of British oppression for his disappointment in Ireland; in fact, he was just plain bored with life on a small farm attending a lonely old lady. After the pattern of ne'er-do-well heirs with well-to-do aunts everywhere, Samuel got impatient and hadn't the tact to cover that up or the character to find himself any other occupation. Aunt Mary wrote:

> *I had promised myself a great deal of pleasure in the company*
> *and society of Your Cousin before he arrived in Ireland but in a*
> *short time I found the reverse he found an acquaintance with a*
> *Clafs of People that did not fit a Man of his discrefstion he*
> *appeared to be innocent and unsuspecting and payed attention*

*to all the tittle triffles that People told him and in a Short time
grew carelefs about me and seemed uneasy to get away he
complained much of my method of liveing and thought I did not
give him enough of Money. I provided him in a suite of Cloaths
which I suppose you had an opportunity of seeing and Kept him
in every other article I thought he required and all did not please
so I was reconciled to let him return to that land so highly
favoured and enjoy all those luxiorys that flows from plenty
liberty and peace.*

It cuts two ways, of course. Aunt Mary's sarcasm about "that
land so highly favoured" and her justification that she "Kept him
in every other article I thought he required" suggest that a bossy
old lady tried to direct a grown man in ways she had no right
to—and when she failed, she dealt with him with high words and
the Stewart sneer.

When Aunt Mary and Samuel at last exploded into mutual
condemnation and Samuel determined to leave Killinchy, Aunt
Mary says:

*I had a letter wrote to you and put into your Cousins Chist
when he returned to Ammerica but in Consequence of some
parts of his conduct I did not approve of John Stewart thought
proper to take it from him in Belfast and for the very reason I
will tell you of—Your father being a favorite Brother of my
Sister Janes and her never haveing it in her power to make any
acknowledgement to him when liveing left to me a Bed Quilt
which I intended to send to Sister Nancy and the numbers of a
New Testament my Brother had got before he died all which I
intended to send to you and had the Letter wrote and all packed
up to send away when he refused to carry them and We thought
it the better way to stop the Letter when he would not take the
goods. . . .*

One can see the scene: Aunt Mary, wearing a mutch cap and
shawl, standing in the kitchen of "the Newhouse" her brother

had built—or perhaps confronting Samuel, having climbed slow-ly and carefully up the stairs to the front bedroom where Samuel was now throwing clothes into an open trunk with just-restrained violence. The house, that of a prosperous tenant farmer, would be built of stone—two storys, white plastered—with a slate roof, and there would be a kitchen and a parlor downstairs on each side of the hall and two or three low-ceilinged bedrooms upstairs. Samuel, thin and wiry with spikes of lank black hair and the bony Stewart face, glares at Aunt Mary. He is at bay now, for he feels cheated of an inheritance and the full life he thinks he had been owed. Ireland, as he sailed across the ocean, had seemed like the harbor where his ship would come in at last, but it turned out, instead, to be his last chance; he failed—or in his mind *was* failed—as sadly and badly as ever.

Many men had come to America because "rents, tithes and taxes" indeed frustrated them, but Samuel was frustrated by his own nature, and it was hard in America, the land of infinite op-portunity, to admit this. In Ireland Samuel thought he would be at home. Aunt Mary was sharp, however, and she knew when he was slackening off on the farm.

Far more onerous were her demands for attention to herself. When Samuel at night wandered into Killinchy to the tavern, Aunt Mary waited up with a candle—burning pence as the tal-low dripped. The first time he was touched, the second time he was surprised and a little nettled. Suddenly aware of her watch-ing and waiting, he wanted to go more often to the tavern to get away from her, but he hadn't the coins to go more often. She, who would probably have given him money for anything he wanted to do at home, would give him no more to go to the tav-ern ("He found an acquaintance with a Clafs of People that did not fit a Man of his discrefstion . . . and in a Short time grew carelefs about me and seemed uneasy to get away. . . ."). She, re-membering her Brother James's devotion to the invalid sister Jean, was hurt in the weary way of an aching old wound. Once again she was more useful than loved. But this time, no, it wouldn't happen. *She* had the farm, she had the money, and this stranger from the New World, who stood glowering over his trunk so different from the figure of her hopes, would not be indulged by her. ("And so I was reconciled to let him return to that land so highly favoured. . . .")

But she wanted to send tokens out to the only family she had left in the World, Old or New, and who were so far away they might as well be with her parents and brothers and sister in Heaven. "I am indeed in a Dessolate situation divested entirely of my near relation," Aunt Mary reflected and appeared in the low door of Samuel's bedroom, with her brother's "Numbers of a new Testament" (pamphlets of each book of the New Testament printed and bound separately) and the bed quilt Sister Jean had made. Samuel, frustrated and hurt himself (he never realized that his dependence on people to give him a sense of purpose in life first appealed, then wearied them), smothered by Aunt Mary's hopes, saw the bulky, smothering quilt on her arm and said, "No! I will not carry that." It was ridiculous, he thought; the quilt seemed to him the emblem of all the domesticity and gentility and dribbling away of life in slops from a teapot and chaff from a wheat crop that an old lady fussed about. The quilt was not a thin patchwork like those on the frontier, scrapped together and not sufficient but essential for warmth in an unheated log house. This quilt was plump with goosedown and scored with tiny stitches like the overcultivated little fields of Aunt Mary's farm, regular in their borders of stone fencing ("Land is so well cultivated in this country . . . although the farms is small."). This quilt was a comforter and Samuel wanted no comfort—he wanted satisfaction. "I will not carry that," he said.

Aunt Mary's chin trembled a bit from the force of this blow; the frill of her cap quivered. "But, nephew, they will be packed to travel with you at no tra-able"—her voice shook over the broad Irish a—"to yourself."

"Damme"—Samuel crashed the top of his horsehair trunk down—"I will not carry the tracts and tea cosys of an old woman across the waters. You have put me to all expense and trouble for more than a year—and now you want me to carry your bit pieces, like a tinker, to America for you. If you give me the money for a carrier, I'll take the packet—otherwise I cannot manage." He lifted the trunk itself, moving it unnecessarily, and crashed it down.

"I should think you've had money enough out of me to hire six carriers"—Aunt Mary was on her high horse now, her mouth pursed tighter in the plump face—"you're entirely too grand a carrier for me yourself. I can pay no more."

("I never sent for him for any other purpose than to acknowledge him something and certainly would have had he behaved himself and settled at home with me he still complained for want of money and that was what I had not to give him.")

Downstairs in the kitchen, Aunt Mary's hired man, Mathew Fulton, a stocky young fellow with a thatch of brown hair, and the maidservant, a Catholic girl whose blue eyes twinkled at Mathew, both jumped and grinned at each other when the trunk hit the floor above. Mathew squeezed the servant girl's shoulders as he scuttled from the room to the stableyard. Aunt Mary pampered her men and bullied her maids unmercifully; it wouldn't do that they should be caught together. ("I always live as usual and my Friend Mathew Fulton and a Girl is all my family.")

Samuel, grandiosely hiring a cart for the chunky little trunk that he could have carried on his shoulder, left "the Newhouse" that sat perhaps at right angles to the old cottage at the end of the lane from which Aunt Mary's brothers had left for America. He left sometime in the spring or summer—daffodils may have dappled the green of the home meadow, or perhaps the lusher vibrant green of July absorbed the darting cries of rooks in the sycamores.

"Good-bye, aunt." Samuel sullenly flung himself into the cart and was driven off, burning inside with so sharp an anger and hurt it was as though he had swallowed one of the orange peat turfs that glowed in the kitchen grate when he came back to the Newhouse late from the tavern. Aunt Mary stood at the parlor window watching him with no tears—or one perhaps for herself—but feeling dull and tired. In January she wrote, sitting at the same parlor window where sycamores now showed skeletal and the meadow was frostbound, "Here we have no continuing city, no sure place of abode and . . . 'tis one continuing changeing scene from the cradle to the grave."

Aunt Mary was worried the next year, 1826, because she had not heard from anyone in America:

I hope there is no prejudice in your mind against me in Consequence of Your Cousin Samuel not likeing either my mode or proceeding to him or the Country while he stoped for be ashured that I did not send for him in Order to put him to any expense on my account to satisfy my curiosity in seeing him . . . from the manner in which I was left I thought he would be a comfort to me and a benefit to himself in the end. But I soon found that self interest was his principal design.

For Aunt Mary the seasons pursued their regular course: "Last summer was remarkably dry and warm with us and our Oats crops . . . felt the effts of it." But the rotation of the earth was not comfort enough in the face of oblivion.

Her last letter ends not with hopes of heaven nor gratitude for mercies on earth, but with a flat statement of death: "If you have any opportunity you may let James Marchall know that his Cousin Robt Marchall . . . is dead 1 March." Then on the outside of the letter, she makes one last gesture to ward off the dark and addresses the letter to "Mr. Samuel Stewart Son of the Late Jas Stewart." It is as if she identifies Samuel not as captain of the militia, elder of the church, and landowner, but as his father's son, so that his father—and she—will not disappear completely from the earth.

When Aunt Myra died 140 years later, after the funeral and supper at my grandparents', my grandfather, who was executor of the will, insisted we all drive back into town to Aunt Hallie's big house on Sixth Avenue, where he would read the will. My mother had protested against going back to Aunt Myra's own bleak house to read—although Grandfather, with his devotion to ritual and tradition, wanted to do that—so we listened attentively in Aunt Hallie's living room with the gold paper on the walls, while Grandpa stood erect in his black suit with the fringe of hair at the back of his head making a little round pad above his thin neck. When he had finished reading Myra's bequests to her sisters and Mother (child of her dead sister Jean), Mother said, "Well, that's a relief. There's nothing in there for Bill Lochran."

"Indeed and you're right about that, Lucy," said Aunt Hallie in her best mock Irish accent.

I remembered the warmth of the man in the leather jacket at lunch the day of the franks and beans, and later I asked my mother why she disliked Bill Lochran so much. "He took advantage," she said. "Sometimes older women get a mother complex about a young man and he was very good-looking—"

"He made"—Father said with indignation—"he made Myra turn in a perfectly good Dodge for an old secondhand Cadillac." Father had always wanted a Cadillac himself.

I found out from my parents that they thought Bill Lochran apple-polished Myra and got her to take pity on him because he had no place to live after he graduated from high school. At that time Myra and her oldest sister Mabel were sharing a big old house in Pittsburgh, bought by Myra, where Mabel was supposed to keep house and take in boarders as a means of earning her own keep. Mabel had never found a purpose in life, and the other sisters had cast her off one by one. Myra and Mabel were not getting along when Myra brought Bill to stay. Mabel blew up, turned sarcastic, and eventually refused to speak to Myra. Myra, however, with the obstinacy of her infatuation—and simplicity (she could, perhaps, be such a severe woman because she was quite simple emotionally)—refused to give Bill up.

"Why, we went there for dinner one night, and the two

of them wouldn't talk to one another," Father said, shaking his head.

Later I found, among Myra's things, an envelope of notes on small pieces of blue and yellow paper, carefully held together with a rubber band and preserved. They said such things as *Mabel, William is sleeping and will not get up until noon as he worked the night shift. Please do nothing to awaken him*, or *Mabel, William is not in yet. Please do not lock the door.*

Father said, "I've read in the Bible about people who were possessed of the Devil, but I never believed it possible until I saw your Aunt Mabel that night. She wouldn't talk to Myra, but every time Myra came in or out of the room, Mabel would hiss at her just like a snake."

"She didn't just hiss. Tell him what she did." Mother was rarely this candid, and, as though afraid of stopping herself, she continued immediately, "When Aunt Myra came near her, Aunt Mabel would say 'shit ass' again and again."

!!!

I was dumbfounded. It was inconceivable. Those old ladies—Myra ponderous and solemn with her thick blue hair, Mabel whom I remembered with flyaway hair, green eyes, and a hollow face, Myra perhaps standing by a maroon portiere that would frame a dark oak doorway, Mabel sitting kinetically on the edge of a straight chair cursing and hissing—I couldn't imagine at their most tortured that they would pull through the fabric of convention with clawing words, flourishing them in a witch dance. But then I also couldn't imagine them knowing—or, more to the point, feeling—anything about sex.

On the feeling point I was obviously wrong. It had been shortly after this dinner, apparently, that Mabel fell down the stairs of that house, nearly killing herself and paralyzing her right side. She claimed, sometimes, that Myra had pushed her, although this was very doubtful. Even in an argument about Bill Lochran Myra's strongest weapon would be heavy words. When I was an adult I asked my mother once again about Aunt Mabel's fall, and she said Mabel claimed that she was trying to protect

Myra from a sexual assault by Bill Lochran. Again, one can see Mabel, consumed with frustration and jealousy, wandering perhaps into Bill Lochran's room; his waking, her backing from the door; his asking what she wanted; her backing off the top step; the cry and waves of white nightgown and Medusa hair plunging down the stairwell.

Myra, as I knew, continued to see Bill Lochran long after Mabel recovered and they split up their household, Myra returning to Parnassus and the dingy house on the hill where I found her. After her death I found, sorting and organizing and often just piling daguerreotypes, eighteenth-century letters, and 1920s Brownie snapshots, that materials relating to the same subject were not necessarily together. A few days after I had found the notes that Myra left Mabel, I found folded together in an envelope four medium-sized pieces of rather fuzzy grayish notepaper covered with typing. The first sheet began:

This is an account of the money Bill Lochran borrowed from me
which is covered by my securities at the Mellon National Bank
New Note 10 Mar. 1952. . . . . $1300.00
Interest on this money $9.10

The list of principal and interest, always noting "not paid," continued onto a second page:

Balance due 13 Nov. 1953. . . . . $1392.36

This continued down a long column of figures to:

Balance due 13 July 1956 (No paymnt) $1367.07

The third sheet had a paragraph of writing at the top:

On Monday February 26, 1951 Bill had a bad accident with
his car in Duquesne and was taken to the McKeesport hospital.
The car was taken to Peckman's garage in McKeesport for

*repair. At that time the Lochrans were expecting their first child.
If I had not borrowed the money and loaned it to Bill he would
have lost his car, and he would not have had any way to get to
and from work on the Railroad. He was on extra board most of
the time so that he might not know from day to day where he
would work. During the time his car was being repaired, I
allowed him to use my car and did without the use of my car
myself so that he could get to work.
I borrowed this money on my life insurance policy from the
Union Mutual Life Insurance Co., and Peckman was paid
April 28, 1951. This is a record of what he has paid on the debt
and what he still owes:*

There then followed, as usual, a long column of figures and the
usual notation: "No payment made since 16 Dec, 53." The final
sheet of paper contained two paragraphs of writing:

*On 20 November 1953 without my consent because of what he
owed me, he traded cars at an expense of $460.00 which he
borrowed with his usual promise that he would not fail to pay
all, if I would go along with his proposition. I was in the hospital
at that time and not in a position to oppose his plan. This
money was paid to Associates Discount Corporation, and he
has not made any payment on this money.*

Mary Stewart to Samuel Stewart, January 4, 1825: "I never
sent for him for any other purpose than to acknowledge him
something. . . . He still complained for want of money and that
was what I had not to give him."

When I had read Aunt Mary's letters, I put the two packs together. For one crazy minute I thought that perhaps Aunt Myra
had invented Aunt Mary, the sister of her great-great-grandfather. The past seemed so much in her possession that who was
to say she had not projected and carefully counterfeited, calling
up almost as an act of will those old letters as she had carefully
typed out the grievances she owed Bill Lochran and the debts of

money he owed her. But no, Mary, the anagram of Myra, was just the same point on the endless cycle of human need coming around 120 years earlier.

> *20 February he borrowed $90.00 to hold the lease on the house he moved into that spring. I told him positively that I could not let him have the money. He insisted that he could not hold the lease for the house without this money and that if I would let him have it, he would pay it back in a short time, and pay up the other money he owed. At that time they were expecting their child, and consideration for his wife influenced me.*

The touching transparency of self-justification: "and consideration for his wife influenced me."

INTERLUDE

WHEN I thought of Aunt Myra in later years and her terrible needs, I always thought of Bill Lochran's hands. Those thick, white, smooth hands, with their jagged nails as they hung down between his knees when he sat on the edge of his chair or when he fed her, affected me the way his smile did. I knew that I had been interested in him in the same way Aunt Myra was. And I knew then that it was both right and terribly wrong for me to think of him as I did and to want to push the thought of the little strawberry girl from my mind.

The other thing I came to notice was that, mostly, love was something you yearned for or imagined with someone who didn't return it—Aunt Myra and Bill Lochran, Aunt May and Mr. Love, Aunt May and Aunt Charlotte. With the exception of Quint and Ruby, between whom sexual tension crackled in little spurts of annoyance even when they were old, most of the people I knew were in relationships that were as restrictive and supportive as an old-fashioned corset.

"I love your father *much more* than he has ever loved me," my mother would say in moments of anger. Since this was coupled with her dictum of "Never a cross word!" it was hard to know what feelings at all were moving between them.

* * *

When I was about fifteen years old the Kincaid aunts were to come to Cedar Hill, where we lived by then, for a holiday dinner at Christmastime. The aunts, of course, had never owned a car, so they were coming with their best friend, Maisie McCreight, who drove a high old Dodge with the iridescent blue surface of a faded satin dress. This particular December night when Maisie McCreight's old car pulled up in front of our house, which was bedecked to a fare-thee-well with seasonal paraphernalia, only Aunt May and Maisie got out. "Where's Charlotte?" we asked in amazement. "She didn't want to come," May said calmly. "She said she'd be home by four o'clock and if she was too late—she was helping with a year-end audit at the church—she'd stay at home or take the bus."

A half hour later Charlotte called in tears. She had gotten home at 4:05, she had gone back to the church to see if they were waiting for her there (the building was closed by then), and she had taken a taxi to the bus station only to find that the buses were on holiday schedule and the next one didn't go until seven. The bus trip took an hour and a half and involved a change in downtown Pittsburgh.

The upshot was that Charlotte, hellbent on not missing a Christmas treat, arrived at the end of the busline in Cedar Hill in floods of tears at eight-thirty. Through it all May was serene and even made little jokes.

At times she hated Charlotte, and despite being her sister and housemate for sixty-five years, she would do her an injury. No one died and there were no physical consequences, but we made May and Charlotte into amusing characters because otherwise their lives were too painful to see.

That was the truth, and it was not one that anybody could live with.

GETTING AWAY

Because we moved away from Parnassus to Cedar Hill before I went to high school I had a certain distance about Parnassus—the distance of a theatergoer sitting in a favorite seat on the aisle watching the shenanigans of a familiar but still deeply stirring old melodrama. But eventually, after college, I knew that I had to get farther away than Cedar Hill, farther away than Pittsburgh. At college, in New England, my roommate had once said, "Everybody here is trying to get away from their past, but you carry the whole thing on your back."

When I moved, I went as far as I could get—spiritually—and still be in America. That was when I moved to the most predictable counterpoint to the small-town virtues and terrors of Parnassus—New York City, of course.

But I was not willing to give up my Parnassus precedents, and when I moved as a young man in the 1970s I thought I had two to rely on.

My father had gotten his "fifth-year" degree (as Ruby always called a master's degree) at New York University, my mother regarding that as a plot of May's to keep him from staying at home and getting married. That was when he had stayed at the Earle Hotel on the northwest corner of Washington Square. He wore white linen suits out of doors and, wearing no suit at all, studied in a bathtub full of cold water when the temperature climbed above ninety; he enjoyed the new Radio City Music Hall, where he could sit in the second balcony and smoke his cigar, the thin white brush stroke of smoke curling upward while he watched the Rockettes kick their thirty pairs of white legs; and he enjoyed Yankee Stadium.

He had been conned by Mr. Dargeon, the elegant old bachelor with the scheme for getting rich—for *somebody* getting rich, only as it turned out it was himself, not Chauncey. But even that had been an experience not all bad. Father quoted him for the rest of his life ("Dargeon always said you can't be an honest man and be president of the United States"—interesting observation from him), and he had learned about French restaurants and breathed a cosmopolitan air.

The other family precedent I had for taking on New York was my grandfather's attendance in 1951 at the Presbyterian General Assembly as the representative for Redstone Presbytery, of which Parnassus was a member. The meetings had been held in the Fifth Avenue Presbyterian Church, a red sandstone building with a gilded clock in its steeple, standing in the imposing row of the University Club and Saint Thomas's Church on Fifth Avenue. When I first moved to New York I went to church regularly and, because my grandfather had recommended this church, I went there. It was designed in exactly the same plan as the Parnassus Presbyterian Church with sloping golden oak pews lapping around the pulpit in broad semicircles like waves at sunset around an unscalable promontory.

When I went home for Christmas the first year I asked my grandfather where he had stayed while he attended the General Assembly. "The St. Regis Hotel," he told me. "My goodness," I said, brushed already with city snobbery, "that's very ritzy." "Oh yes." He gave a cavalier wave of the hand. "There was a great deal of this business"—and he mimed a flunky bowing to left and right.

When I started to work I told the editor of the smart art magazine where I'd landed a job that I was attending the Fifth Avenue

Presbyterian Church because my grandfather recommended I go there. I also once mentioned that I made oatmeal for myself for breakfast, and the editor exclaimed, himself a handsome crippled man not much older than I, "You're a boy! A mere boy adrift in the canyons of the city!"

Those precedents tied me to the past, fondly but nevertheless for real. But there was another precedent, much farther back and yet much closer to me in a way, that might have shown me how to break away.

Aunt Myra had, among her archives, a small stamped leather packet, which, when opened, showed the solemn, handsome face of a young man staring out from a glimmering surface, as from a mirror. The face belonged to Robert McGahan, the half-brother of my great-grandmother, and the photograph was a daguerreotype. When Aunt Myra had first shown it to me she had said in her *ex cathedra* way, "*That* is a real daguerreotype." In New York City alone in 1855 the *New York Tribune* estimated that there were three million photographs taken. These were almost without exception portrait photographs. One such portrait was taken at Rees & Co., No. 585 Broadway, and posted to a log cabin perched on the hill above a gristmill on Puckety Creek, four miles from Parnassus.

Robert McGahan's face with its long dark hair, high forehead, and large, deep-set brown eyes had to be caught with a half-turn of the wrist as you held the little case with its red velvet and yellow gilt lining. The surface mirrored my own face, drawn into Robert's, if the light struck the silver surface in a certain way.

"That young man ran away to New York when he was fourteen years old." Aunt Myra told me that while he was there, he stowed away on a ship and sailed to England, where he saw Queen Victoria. "When he came back"—Aunt Myra's stories were always vividly succinct—"he dove into New York Harbor to save a little boy who had fallen off a steamship and, although he rescued both the child and himself, he died of pneumonia several weeks later."

Years later I found a popular novel of the 1930s in which a

young hero stowed away on a ship bound for England and while he was there saw Queen Victoria, so that part of Robert's saga may have been another example of Aunt Myra's determination to turn the family past into romance. But I also found among the papers in the trunks I gathered when Aunt Myra died two letters from the 1850s about Robert and two letters written to Myra in the 1930s from Greenwood Cemetery in Brooklyn confirming the site of his grave. At least some of Robert's life was romantic enough.

The cabin, grown into a farmhouse, which he had run away from, was on the Greensburg Road, which led from Parnassus to the Ludwick farm. It reared up on the right with a porch above a bank covered with honeysuckle that hung over the road. "The number of times," my mother would say in a disgusted voice, "that I have heard 'Your grandmother was born in that house' from Aunt Myra—if I had a penny for every one . . ."

My grandfather made no such remark as we drove by. Robert was connected to the Stewarts, not to his family, yet his life pursued the course and tradition of Robert's as surely as Puckety Creek wound through its stony bed to the river. Between Quint's purchase of the slim blue book of definitions and usage, entitled *Better Say*, which he bought in 1905, and Robert's last letter, there was a gap of fifty-one years. The same urge drove them both. Robert McGahan was three generations removed from the Scots-Irish peasant who first staked out land in the wilderness on Pine Run, near James Stewart's land. By the time of Robert's youth, the hilly Pennsylvania farms had been securely in possession of their European-descended owners for more than fifty years. The farms returned a poor living for incessant, heavy labor. In a country whose manifest destiny it was to settle a whole continent to the West and where technology was exploding with opportunities in the East, there were always possibilities, however.

Robert's mother, Sarah Dickey McGahan, had married as her second husband Jacob Alter, one of a twelve-branched clan of Swiss German immigrants. Jacob ran the sawmill and gristmill at Alters' Mills, which supplemented the farm income, and the homestead, because of the comings and goings to the mill, was a community center as well. Still, there was only a poor living to be had with Puckety Creek often going dry. Sarah and Jacob's marriage, although it was a second one for each, lasted nearly forty years, and in that time they moved from Alters' Mills to various locations on new farms in Ohio. Sarah took with her each time a heavy, machine-made bedstead and bedroom suite (pronounced "suit") of mahogany, high headboard pointed in Gothic Revival style, and the bed labeled on the inside with a broad pencil: *Sarah A. D. Alter, her bed.*

It was perhaps this bed—one of a kind manufactured by New England factories in the thousands in the 1850s—and the marriage it celebrated that precipitated Robert's flight from home. His father, Sarah's first husband, had died in the late 1840s, succumbing to one of those diseases—ague, appendicitis—that felled strong men in the course of a week.

So the handsome, serious young man ran away, creeping from the bed he shared with Alter stepbrothers one black night before the cock crew and the farm began to stir at dawn. He wrapped some heavy bread cut off the loaf in the kitchen and some cold meat in his bandanna handkerchief and stole down the lane to the mill by the creek. He may have followed the creek to the river and either hitched a ride on a flatboat taking produce to the markets at Pittsburgh, or followed the riverbank itself to the metropolis. From Pittsburgh Robert could have simply worked his way East, helping farmers for a day's board and sleeping in haystacks, or he may have worked in the city—where he would have been as remote from his family 25 miles away as if it were 250 miles—until he could save the fare to ride on the new Pennsylvania Railroad that had connected Pittsburgh to Philadelphia in 1850.

In whatever way, Robert made his way to New York, a New York where the population of nearly 600,000 had doubled in the decade between 1840 and 1850, where the gridiron of streets and avenues was regularly stamped on the island north of Washington Square like broadsides turned out by a printing machine. In

New York Robert intended to make his mark, and in the best American tradition first set up by Benjamin Franklin arriving in Philadelphia with only a roll in his pocket: He started in the printing business with aspirations toward a writer's career.

On April 15, 1854, after he had been away from home for at least a year, Robert wrote to his mother from the "*Express* Office, cor of Wall and Nassau St":

> *Dear Mother:*
>
>   *. . . In some future letter I shall give you a long account of my doings for the last year; in the present I will confine myself to my present position, and speculations as to my future prospects. . . . I think I have the natural talents, if I only cultivate them, to command, at some future day, an honored position in society.*

Then, the Presbyterian conscience hovering over him, Robert forestalls his mother's clucking tongue: "I know, there is a passage in Holy Writ reading as follows: 'A fool is wise in his own conceit,' " but he continues, urged on by his heady self-reliance: "I may say that I have gained some reputation as a writer, already, for some of the New York papers. . . . If you should ever meet with any composition in any newspaper you are reading, signed as follows you may be sure that I wrote it. This is the signature: 'R. Maxwell M.' "

Robert continued his letter, boasting, complaining, and as unsure about his direction as any college sophomore in a later generation.

> *I feel the need of a better education, very much, and intend to contrive some means by which I can acquire a better knowledge of some branches of which I am very much in want. The printing business is very unhealthy; and I will quit it as soon as I can get anything else that I can do as well at. I feel the effects of it on my system already. But I cannot make up my mind altogether to go West, and adopt a farmer's life. . . .*

Mrs. Alter wasn't happy with her son, either, when he was at home, it seems:

You remember when I was at home to visit you last how loth I was to make myself useful about the farm; you blamed me with being lazy; and I do not wonder very much at you for so doing. But the fact of the matter is, I have been used to a light, easy occupation for so long, that I cannot engage, with my whole heart in a heavy toilsome one. Not that I am lazy; for my reason tells me that I am not, when engaged in my own business. But farming, hauling rails, rolling logs, husking corn, building fence, etc., is just as much out of my sphere, as cutting wood and feeding the threshing machine is out of yours. I make these few suggestions merely to erase from your mind any false impression which you may have in regard to me in this particular.

This slightly stiff young man who wanted his mother's approval so badly seemingly had as alternatives the resources of a new continent. Burgeoning industry and rolling prairie both required only energy, it appeared, for a man to mine riches beyond his wildest dreams. Robert had every reason to expect that his youth and the cunning he had acquired in his picaresque progress from Alters' Mills to the *Express* office would lead him to success. He reassures his mother, who must have laboriously scrawled her concern to him, writing with one of the new steel-tipped pens, tongue clenched between the wooden dentures she obviously wears in her tintype "likeness":

You spoke in your letter about my youthfulness and on account of it feared to have me traveling around so much. [Was Aunt Myra right: Did he stow away on a ship bound for England?] *On this point I will say a few words. When I was first thrown on my own resources, I was, it is true very young; I had no experience in the ways of the world, and consequently felt my tender age. It is a good while since then. Since I first*

started out in the world, I have been thrown on my own
resources and have been taught many severe lessons. I suppose
that I have had as much experience in life, as any person in
your neighborhood of twice my age. Although I am not yet 18, I
have seen a great deal of this world, and I hope I have profited
thereby.

The shock of finding out that that serious face in the polished, elusive daguerreotype—which could pass for twenty-five and earnestly intended to do so—was "not yet 18" is countered by the fact that Robert's contemporaries also thought he was older:

I pass for a journeyman, everywhere, now, and have for a long
time back, and none of those working with me, nor my
employers, suspects but that I am 21; I am a good workman,
and do as much as any hand my employers have got, except two
or three extraordinarily good ones; and do more than the
majority of them. As long as I do this, it is nobody's business
what my age is; though if it was suspicioned that I was so young
it might injure me. But no one knows it, and no one here ever
shall know it.

When I was a child my mother would say, quoting her mother, the pale, long-faced Jean Stewart whose death had elevated her to oracular status: "Experience keeps a dear school but fools will learn in no other." Jean, I later found out, was herself quoting Benjamin Franklin's smug "Poor Richard" (and using *dear* in the archaic sense of expensive, as the French still use *cher*). Well, Robert McGahan seemed to feel that experience, dearly bought, would stand him in better stead than years, statically accumulated on the farm. He told his mother, "In my opinion, it is not age that renders a person capable of enduring the storms and rebuffs of the world; it is *experience*." He then indicated he was sending some money home—ready cash was always in short supply on the farm and at the mill, where the miller took payment "in kind," usually a portion of the grain he ground. Robert re-

quested in closing that "you . . . give my kind regards to all en-
quiring friends."

But a year later the friends had no more reason to enquire.
Robert was dead.

We don't know how the news reached the farm, whether
neighbors trooped in bearing pies and chickens one day and then
came back, wearing dusty Sunday black for a funeral service—
with no body—the next. Or whether, perhaps, Mrs. Alter bore
her grief quietly, more or less alone; her son had been one of
many, and stepbrothers and a grim, busy stepfather would hardly
notice that Robert was gone for good. But we do know pretty exactly how Robert died and what he thought as he was dying.

Secret Societies were the fad for young typesetters as well as
college boys, and a fellow member of Robert's Secret Society
wrote a long-winded masterpiece of Victorian prose to Robert's
mother describing her boy's last moments ("a history of your son,
so far as it might be possible, in view of my connection with
him"). The letter wallows in the Victorian cult of death ("It is
strange that he who a few short weeks before was with us in com-
parative health and vigor, should then have been a lifeless
clod,—yet so it was"), and it scales peaks of high-mindedness
aided by appropriate poetry and biblical quotation. The calligra-
phy is elegant and the punctuation—usually ignored by country
correspondents altogether—is perfect.

The picture of Robert that emerges is of a boy determined to
advance himself, intensely serious about himself, and who is only
saved from being an unbearable prig by his gusto for life. Be-
moaning the suddenness of Robert's death, C. Corson, Mrs. Alter's correspondent, says that it was "but three short weeks before
his death" that Robert raised his voice "deep and loud . . . in ad-
vocacy of a question of moral right and conduct . . . in denuncia-
tion of what seemed dishonorable." Mr. Corson continues to say
that it took "time and close observation" to understand Robert
because his "singularities and eccentricities" made him many
enemies and not many friends. Then Corson, who says that he
knows Robert to have been "unsurpassed in his devotion as a

friend," begins nonetheless to heap up Robert's undesirable qualities. Although one of his favorite studies was elocution, Robert, "being of violent temperament, unfortunately . . . was totally unfitted for a debater." Corson continues rather doubtfully, "against the purity of [Robert's] character I say, as Christ said to the persecutors of the abandoned woman, '*let him who hath no sin, cast the first stone.*' " But worst of all by far, he suggests that Robert had *religious doubts.*

It must have given Mrs. Alter some comfort that her son had such erudite friends. But it ultimately may have brought more pain than comfort because from what Mrs. Alter could puzzle out, spectacles on her nose, sitting by the "betty lamp," Robert's friend said that he, Robert, had been "skeptical" in his religious beliefs. And more than skeptical, he had suffered in a "labyrinth of doubt" (What was a labby-rinth? she wondered. No matter— she knew doubt as an enemy all too well) and even—Heavenly days!—it seemed that Robert had been "atheistical." Mrs. Alter fell back in her rocker, her mouth trembling over her wooden denture.

To lose a fine son in this life was bad enough, but to lose him to eternal perdition in the next was cruelly sad and more than a mother could bear.

Mrs. Alter behaved with dignity and had written that she wanted to pay Robert's funeral expenses. Mr. Corson took umbrage, however, and answered: "My dear Madam . . . permit me to suggest as touching more material things . . . that the expenses of Robert's funeral (which, by-the-bye, was got up in very respectable style, such as I should wish for myself,) have been entirely defrayed by one or two, who would, I am certain, reject any return of the amount, as intimated, if they did not feel themselves insulted by the offer."

He then embellished with delight the desolation in which Robert had died: "No Mother was by to soothe his aching brow, no sister's care could lighten any pain, no father's counsel e'en was his, no brother's kindness could contribute to his wants, *all,*

all, were left to be supplied by those who were in fact, in one sense at least, strangers to him."

Finally, in a postscript, Corson gives one last twist of the knife to the Alters' social adequacy. With tact as heavy as one of print-ing presses Robert used to compose type at the *Express*, he asks: "My Mother begs me to suggest that she has, as yet, no answer to her letter, (to you) written almost immediately after Robert's death. Did her's miscarry? or has your answer."

Mrs. Alter saved both Robert's last letters and Corson's epistle. Her sense of guilt about not being present at Robert's deathbed would not have been so severe as it might have today simply because it was impossible for her to get there. There was no way of notifying her; the telegraph had only just reached from New York to Pittsburgh, and the time needed and expense of the journey made it unthinkable. Corson's heavy hacking away at Mrs. Alter's feelings may have thrown her off, and she may have been either humbly impressed—or, more likely, embarrassed, flushing dull red under the sunburn she had acquired by August, despite her best efforts to wear a sunbonnet and keep a lady's complexion—by his implacable pricking of the undeveloped muscle of etiquette. But sorrow is a pure emotion. It was Robert's loss she minded.

Corson's letter was a genteel curiosity for Mrs. Alter, a hair picture or a feather wreath like her girls worked for the parlor walls on winter afternoons when the light was good enough; in fact, the letter resembled one of those pen-and-ink mourning pictures that had been popular twenty years earlier, showing a gangly figure weeping across a grave under a willow, and it was just as commemorative and decorative and divorced from Robert himself as those pictures. The letter that has tearstains blotched across the ink, making brown freckles on its tan surface, is Robert's, not his friend's.

Of Robert himself, it is hard to know a lot. Corson, self-designated as a "pious friend," says of Robert's "atheistical" ten-dencies that he found a paper where Robert expressed those doubts. The last lines of it run: "To him in whose path thorns have been scattered, death loses half its terrors. He reflects that if he, so far as lay within his power has well performed his task, *he can be no worse off after death. Such is my case*—Robert McGahan."

So Robert was driven and sensitive—that most torturous of combinations in which the victim of his own perceptions sees what is lacking in his world ("I feel the need of a better education very much"), but winces so acutely that he pauses at the sensation of every inadequacy he yearns to overcome. His chest was weak, he was pale, he described typesetting as both "easy and light" and "very unhealthy." His passions burned; his thirst for recognition was unquenchable—he was a hero—he jumped in the river to save a drowning child; he caught a cold and died. And that, except for his mother's cherishing two letters and a silvery daguerreotype, is all.

Except that it would never have happened anywhere but in the land of infinite opportunity. Horace Greeley, sitting bald, bewhiskered, eccentric, and brilliant, in the offices of the *New York Herald Tribune* on up Broadway from Robert's *Express* office, wrote "Go West, Young Man" and that seemed to apply equally to "go East." Opportunity, opportunity was all around. It was enough to drive a man like Robert mad. Everywhere a "glorious future" lay around to be picked up like fruit in a neglected September orchard. Fathers and grandfathers who had subdued savages and carved farms out of the forest left a legacy of achievement that sons took to be a right. The farm gave them identity and a background, but it wasn't enough. And yet, and yet on the land survival was the same as success. The land was there to be grappled with and subdued on a daily basis. When you left the land, that wasn't the case. Trade and the new textile mills in New England, the clothing factories of the cities, offered subsistence to anyone with physical endurance but they were far from offering a guarantee of success. They chewed men up. Farm boys like Robert grew up expecting change and change for the better. They wanted more than the farm but, paradoxically, it had been the golden grain pouring out of Jacob Alter's millstones and the fat cattle in the hill pasture that gave Robert the certainty to tell his mother that "you will be proud that *Mr.* Robert McGahan, *Esq.*, is your son."

INTERLUDE

I WENT to New York with all of the stories intact, including Robert's. What I could not see until after I had lived there for a long time and was not very young anymore, was that Robert did what I didn't have the courage to do for many years. *He* had left his past behind, energetically, running toward the future. He created a whole new self, even using a new name: *R. Maxwell M.*, dear Mother.

I came, long, long years after I first read the letters, to know that I had to live my own life. I came to feel that, although I was nothing without the old stories, I would never be anything unless I made them mine—and moved on.

But it was not until I understood that the family were only people themselves, not embodiments of the law, that I could see myself as whole and separate.

When I understood that, I would finally be myself, however drastically that self strayed from the rules of Parnassus.

And I came to understand that they were not perfect in a very particular way with one very particular revelation.

Part Five

THE FLOOD

THE FLOOD

MOTHER would alternately say, "My father sold all of his stock in 1929 just before the crash—ha! ha!—so we never suffered from the Depression," and "Grandpa lost his job in the Depression."

Ruby said once, late in life when the old family were dying with the turn of each season, "We have never had so bad a year since 1936."

A final defeat of personal aspirations and the defeat of the aspirations of industry and technology came together in 1936. Like Noah in the Bible, there was a flood and Grandpa was washed away. During the week of March 16, 1936, the Allegheny, the Monongahela, and the Ohio River valleys were deluged in the worst flood in recorded history since the French first established Fort Duquesne in 1754. Frozen by an exceptionally cold winter and washed with a sudden spring thaw, the hills all the way up to Port Allegheny and down into West Virginia, which had been deforested ruthlessly for a hundred years and more, did not have enough ground cover to hold and absorb the water. Smooth as stones, the hills shed their waters into the rivers, and the rivers rose and rose.

There were virtually no flood controls in the river valleys, despite the fact that poor people down by the rivers in Pittsburgh had to bail out almost every spring. In towns thrown up hastily in the booms of the previous sixty years sewer lines disgorged into the rivers without filtration. The mills poured their wastes in rust-red streams, almost as broad as the rivers themselves, into the waters.

In the confusion of fact and memory, the disaster for Pittsburgh, "the industrial giant among the big cities of the world," as the *Pittsburgh Sun-Telegraph* put it, and Quint's personal disaster were confounded. The flooded wreck of the Industrial Revolution and the personal wreck of hopes came together in the telling.

Grandfather, of course, kept the newspaper accounts of the flood:

PITTSBURGH SUN-TELEGRAPH
SUNDAY, MARCH 29, 1936

Chronology of the Frightful Week of the Flood:

Here, conveniently on one page, is the story of the Great Flood of 1936—the flood that prostrated Pittsburgh, industrial giant among the big cities of the world. Here is the story of the Week of Catastrophe, a story that opens with Darkening Monday, March 16, and closes on the Seventh Day, sunny Sunday, March 22. Here is a story simply written, set forth chronologically in its appalling and unbelievable detail. This is a page you will want to clip—or save carefully with this entire picture section for reference in later years for the complete story of the Great Flood of 1936.
THE EDITOR.

MONDAY

Heavy rains that fell in Western Pennsylvania sent the five main rivers that flow toward the Ohio creeping up their bank. Melting snow added to the torrents in the Red Bank Creek, the Kiskiminetas, the Conemaugh, the Youghiogheny, the Monongahela, and the Allegheny. . . .

Terror gripped the city as the flood surged about office buildings downtown and homes in the North Side. Deaths mounted every hour. Houses were swept loose from their foundations. . . .

Heroic rescuers tumbled from capsized boats to their deaths. . . . A pistol rang out in Liberty Avenue where a frantic man marooned in a building shot at a boatman who refused to rescue him. . . . Fears of water and flood famines spread over the city. . . .

About three o'clock on the morning of Wednesday, March 18, 1936, the day after St. Patrick's Day, Quint had come into Lucille's bedroom and wakened her. "Come here," he said. "You will never see anything like this again as long as you live." They walked out to the sunporch on the back of the bungalow where their breakfast nook with the matching settle benches hung over the edge of the bluff, looking over all of downtown Parnassus. There, spread below them and spreading more all the time, the silver-black waters of Puckety Creek rocked a little in the wind. Friendly old Puckety Creek shot off white splinters of reflected moonlight as it moved beyond its banks across Freeport Street to the foot of Church Street and around the back of the cemetery and the Parnassus Presbyterian Church. Coming toward the creek from the other direction—and only separated from it by the thin ribbon of the railroad raised on snow-covered white banks—the whole Allegheny River stretched from the little rise where the church sat across Sixth Avenue, Fifth Avenue, across what had once been fields down toward Fourth Avenue, all the way to the foot of the huge hill rising from what had once been the other side of the river altogether. There was only steel gray water, lapping white in the moonlight, with the houses of the town set in it, as though the New Kensington town council, despairing of the inefficiency of old Parnassus, had decided to pave over the old, uneven brick streets, slate sidewalks, and little yards with some corrugated viscous surface. The March-black feathery

branches of the trees were reflected upside down in the church-
yard, making a fringed border to the white austerity of the sanctuary. Three billboards set at an angle by what had been Freeport
Street, just below where Quint and Lucille looked, gave their
messages, TOUR THE USA IN YOUR CHEVROLET, SMOKE LUCKY
STRIKES, and MEET CROWN, WEAR DIAMONDS, doubly—once right
side up, once mirrored in the moonlit water. The silence (Quint
had opened one of the windows a little) rose from the lower part
of the town like steam; there was no early morning train whistle,
no sounds of a milk wagon or a farmer's truck on Freeport Street.
There wasn't even any sound of the creek, making a rushing
noise between its banks as it sometimes did when it was swollen
by the spring freshets. There wasn't any creek, just this broad
lake of water that filled every cranny it could until it had no
place to go. Down toward Pittsburgh, the seven tall stacks of the
West Penn Power plant, rising above the valley like the towers of
a temple to the God of Fire, still smoked lazily, and the wet
muddy stench of river rose to the bungalow breakfast nook.

"Well, you'd better get some breakfast while we still have gas,"
Ruby said. She wore her peach-colored satin housecoat, her
gown, as she called it, and she moved back and forth in the
kitchen, ladling water up out of buckets that she had filled the
day before when the river was rising rapidly and it looked like all
the tap water would be cut off. She made coffee and fried eggs
and thick slices of bacon Vic brought in from the farm and made
toast over the gas flames on the stove because there was no electricity for the toaster. She set three places at the table in the
breakfast nook and carried over an oil lamp she had brought up
from the basement the night before when the electricity went
off. The lamp cast its archaic yellow aura over the white enam-
eled tin of the table surface. Quint had his napkin in the silver
ring; Lucille and Ruby had paper napkins. The lamplight turned
the windows black, but the presence of the water below was
scarcely less pervasive than the lamplight.

"What about the Hamiltons?" Ruby asked Quint.

The big brick house on Sixth Avenue where Uncle Lawndis

Hamilton, Aunt Hallie, and Cousin Jane lived was down on the flat near the river. When Grandfather lost his job as postmaster of Parnassus because the Republicans came into office, Uncle Lawndis had got him his job as bookkeeper at "Standard." So on that morning after St. Patrick's Day when the cold river rose to meet the turbulent little creek across town, one of Quint's first thoughts was for the Hamiltons.

In fact, Quint took the Hamiltons out of their second-story window later that morning in a boat and brought them up to the bungalow. Aunt Hallie said when she was climbing the hill she was so downhearted that if she thought she'd be turned to a pillar of salt like Lot's wife, she'd have looked back and been done with it.

("And Jane bore up without a murmur until she was climbing over the windowsill into the boat and she tore her good stockings and she just cried and cried," Mother said.)

The Hamiltons stayed for three weeks. Ruby was in her element. Being lady bountiful to one of the Stewart sisters was her dream come true. She, the latecomer, the replacement for the sainted Jean, was in the position of dispensing hospitality and shelter to proud Hallie, whose husband had graciously found her husband a job. She, the orphan, was needed by this haughty family who had hardly deigned to notice her existence. Hallie had gone to stay, not with her sister Myra who had said she would get up off her deathbed to blackball Ruby from the Eastern Star, but to stay with Ruby.

After three weeks, when the Hamiltons' house had been cleaned and papered and painted, when the ruined dining room suite they had gone to housekeeping with was replaced by the most expensive Jacobean Revival table and chairs that could be found, their legs swollen with woodworkers' elephantiasis, Hallie swept out the door of the bungalow to go back downtown. As she left she said, "Maybe I can do something for you someday."

And a month later she was held to her offer.

* * *

"Why," I asked Father once when I was in high school, "did Grandpa lose his job at the Standard Sanitary?" And Father, who did not much like his father-in-law, who thought Quint was self-indulgent and a poseur who had spent his life "keeping up a front," nonetheless said, making as little of the question as he could, "Well, you know he was bookkeeper there, and I believe he authorized some funds to be spent that he didn't have the authority for." It seemed a satisfactory and respectable answer, and yet it didn't satisfy, and I had respect only for the speaker, none for what he said.

Later, as I came to know more, I tried again. It was on an autumn trip my parents and I took to an old resort, a hot springs just a hundred miles from Pittsburgh, and Mother and I were walking through a meadow opposite the pillared old hotel that stretched infinitely along the hillside in the narrow valley. In the meadow there was a horse, and Mother said she was afraid of horses, as she always did when she was near them, said she had always been afraid of horses ever since she was a little girl. The idea of horses being a regular enough part of the street scene to inspire chronic fright again opened up a vista into the past for me, as quickly glimpsed as the mountain valleys we had passed on our way to Cumberland Springs. I decided to turn into the opening. "Why did Grandpa leave the Standard Sanitary? What did happen?"

Mother abruptly replied, "Do not ask me. I will never tell you."

But then, a year later when Mother visited me in New York, sitting at the table eating croissants for breakfast in my apartment on Eleventh Street, where I seemed to be an adult removed from my everlasting place in the family picture as a child, I said, again, "Why did Grandpa leave the Standard Sanitary?"

And Mother replied, "He stole five hundred dollars."

The world stopped as she said it. It was like an explosion. It was like drowning after one last glimpse of the world as it was— that which had been stopped with the statement "He stole five hundred dollars." Grandpa, the graven ivory idol of order, plenty, and respectability. Grandpa with his red silk dressing gown (made of rayon), with his pipes and his elegance and his linen napkin in the silver ring, Grandpa was not the comfort of old Parnassus, but the sham of red silk that was synthetic.

Mother, having begun her story, continued in a relentless chronicle voice, full of small facts and details but with no emotional tones of judgment coloring the telling. As in the old chronicles, there was no dramatic structure, cumulatively the facts built to a conclusion as crushing as the cairn of stones on an old Indian burial mound out the Puckety Creek Road.

"You see," Lucille said, "Daddy had this friend named Lewellyn who worked at Standard Sanitary and he was a singer in a quartet at the East Liberty Presbyterian Church downtown. He was Welsh (you can never trust the Welsh)." She shook her head. "Anyway, he was a big, good-lookin' fellow and a beautiful singer. He had something funny wrong with him, though, he had a stutter when he talked but he didn't when he sang. Anyway, Daddy admired him and he thought he was his friend. Well, this Lewellyn asked Daddy to loan him five hundred dollars, and Daddy didn't have it, so he borrowed it from the company." Mother said with the earnestness of a religious witness, "Most people who take money like that, *never* intend to keep it. Ninety-nine percent of the people who take money intend to return it."

"But what happened?"

"Well, about six weeks before all this came out, just before the Flood, Daddy said to me one Saturday, 'Lucille, I could use a little money. Do you think you could borrow five hundred dollars for me?' And I said, 'Sure, if I can,' so I went down to the bank and asked to see Mr. Alter and I said I wanted to borrow five hundred dollars, and that old goat Charley Alter said, 'Why, Lucille, you don't have any collateral.' So I went home and told Daddy and he said, 'Well, don't worry about it,' and I never gave it another thought. Oh, I would have done anything, anything, afterward to have gotten the money, if I'd only known. And Daddy was so good"—she got her beatified look on—"he never said a *thing*, not a word, not that he was disappointed, or anything.

"So, about a month after the flood, Daddy came home one night from work, and he and Ruby went into the bedroom and closed the door, and then after a little while they called me in and I could see Ruby was scared, and Daddy said, 'Lucille, I stole five hundred dollars. I'll have to resign from the Session.' "

There was a pause while I digested this. Outside in Eleventh Street a siren rent the air, and the unquiet mutter of the city moved on.

I asked, "Did he have to resign from the Session?"

"No. Nobody ever knew about it outside of the company. Bless his heart, he never even tried to cover it up and when the auditors came, he just showed them the books and they saw, of course, where there was five hundred dollars gone, and he was so honest he didn't even try to hide it.

"Uncle Lawndis was good and repaid the money. (We paid him back later, of course), and they liked Grandpa so well they just let him quit. But that was when our terrible trouble started. We had to sell the house and Daddy and Ruby went out and lived at the Farm for a year. And I lived at Aunt Hallie's for two years. . . ."

She paused and shook her head, "And that Lewellyn never paid Grandpa back one red cent."

This, then, was where it had all led. Conrad Ludwick's stone mansion house and fat barn reared amid dangers of savages, panthers, and rattlesnakes; Massy Harbison's epic trek, guided by robins, to save her people from the savages; the searing of the soul by the ministers and the iron clamps of doctrine they imposed; the yearnings for more than ceaseless toil behind the plow; Quint's aspirations, his self-help books; Ruby's etiquette, the trappings of prosperity: golf games, bridge, mink coats, and a washing machine, this was where it had all led. The pursuit of happiness turned out to have been a wild goose chase.

Quint had borrowed, embezzled, misappropriated—not even stolen—the money because there was such a discrepancy between his appearance of substantial prosperity and the reality of living from paycheck to paycheck that he was embarrassed to admit he couldn't produce five hundred dollars to save his face when Lewellyn expected it of a man with Quint's style. From Conrad Ludwick, "the King of the Pucketoes," to his great-great-grandson, a helpless embezzler living in a bungalow hung above the banks of the uncontrollable swollen Pucketoes.

"Nobody in town ever knew," said Mother. "I think Ivy Dyse might have known because she had worked at Standard and knew people there, but she never told—which was pretty good, considering how she talks."

And so, now, why do I tell? Because in some way this is the answer. This is what it all meant and what it had come to. Because from the time when Grandpa took me up over the hill when I was four or five to see the foundations of the old log house where he was born and gave me the four blunt-headed nails, from the time I went to the farmhouse for the spectacles, I was searching—both backwards and forwards. I was meant to be something, amount to something. And I did not know what it was. There was an avalanche from the past, there was a deluge inexorable and turgid as the floodwaters that moved down the Allegheny and out from the Pucketoes that swept over me when I was told I was to ride the crest of it. I was to justify the old people, but as in the old Scots catechism there was only justification by faith: "By faith are ye saved not works, lest any man should boast." So my justification was meant to be an act of faith. But it had to be an exploration. I could not meet their image of what should have been and what I should be, any more than Grandpa could meet Lewellyn's demand for five hundred dollars.

And I too would counterfeit.

I loved them, but except by witnessing for them and letting them be known, I could not save them.

As someone once said, there is just one more question: Why do you hate Parnassus? I don't hate it, I don't, I don't. . . .

INTERLUDE

IF I am going to tell about them it is only fair (schoolteachers' child that I am, fair is important) to tell about myself.

When I was nine years old my mother observed, reading in the paper, that the Queen of England was expecting a child. "If I were she I'd have as many as I possibly could," she said.

I said, "She doesn't have anything to do with it, does she? I thought God knew when you were married and put a baby in the woman's stomach."

Two days later I was to play at a piano contest in downtown Pittsburgh for which I'd been nominated by my piano teacher. My father drove me down and, on the way, prompted by my mother before he and I left, he told me the facts of life. Like the good teacher he was, he spoke thoroughly, directly, and rather tersely. He explored no subcategories; it was several years later, for instance, that I learned about wet dreams. He was, however, quite clear about the basics. He said he was telling me because he had had to learn these things in locker rooms and on the street and he didn't want the same to be true for me.

He ended by saying, "And after you've done this with a woman, you'll be disgusted and won't want to have anything to do with her for a while."

Needless to say, his timing was slightly off as far as the piano contest went. I was all over the keyboard, unable to tell one note from another. Still, it had not been easy for him and it was very good of him to do it.

"Take care of your religious obligations first," he used to say, "and then your health and then your money, and everything else will be all right."

That wasn't enough for me.

When I was thirteen, my mother, who found comfort in attention toward me from the aunts and old people and courted it but nonetheless worried about the effect, took me for a car ride that was the mirror image of the one with my father several years earlier.

She said one day, "Come with me. I want to drive out to Oakland," where the University of Pittsburgh thrust its phallic Cathedral of Learning into the sky. When we got there she parked and said, "Now I have to go on an errand. You stay here." I protested and asked where she could possibly be going, but she insisted, firmly, that I stay *in the car*. I had, for a change, nothing to read with me (by her design? I can't remember), and there was a *Redbook* (a subscription given inevitably every Christmas by Maisie McCreight) lying on the seat. I began to browse in it and was stopped in my tracks at an article by a woman who discovered that her husband was a homosexual.

The article discussed homosexuality in all the particulars— with more flourishes than Father had discussed heterosexuality but with the same thorough directness. Mother came back to the car before I had finished. I guiltily flipped a few pages farther on and then threw the magazine down on the seat.

A little later, moth to the flame, I was unable to keep myself from picking it up and reading compulsively on. The piece ended by saying that if your son was putting on an old velvet dress, don't worry, he was probably only pretending to be King Arthur.

I knew deeply differently.

As we drove around the top of the cliff by Duquesne University where the city lay below us to the right and the swollen

Monongahela rolled its oily way on to the Ohio on the left, Mother laughed and said, "What are you reading?"

What she had meant to be a warning, I, of course, found a revelation, perhaps even a directive.

But for many years I did not act on what I knew. Finding grown-up love seemed to be far from a certain thing, as I had observed from the aunts and great-aunts and even parents. So I fulfilled everyone's expectations, I witnessed for them, and stayed alone. But when the point of the inverted pyramid that was the past and the family (so many of them) pressed too deeply into my solitary skull, I sidestepped away.

This is their story. This is not about me. It is about a gallant American spirit that had become obsolete to its own circumstances.

But it is true that with me the end of the line had come.

AT THE END

AFTER Quint lost his job, Ruby sold encyclopedias door to door for a few months—or tried to sell them; she never completed a single sale. Then Quint and Ruby sold their bungalow on Monticello Hill and went to Ohio to run a general store that Quint had bought. "They'll be back within the year," said Aunt Hallie, pulling down her chin cynically, and they were, worse broke than before. That was when Vic gave them a piece of the Farm, the only level field slashed in half by the new county road, and Roscoe and Nannie, cut adrift since their mother had died, built the cottage where they all ended up. Ruby went back to teaching school, and as her bosom and bulk increased, so did her importance until, propelled by her natural forthright energy, she was principal of the Monticello Hill Elementary School.

All of this happened before I was born. It all happened before World War II, which seems to have passed over us as an event of distant interest, never much closer than the Movietone newsreel at the Liberty Theater. Chauncey was too old for World War II. Quint had been too old for World War I. No member of the family had been in a war, since Quint and Roscoe and Vic's father, Robert Dinsmore, marched off to fight the johnny rebs in

Texas in 1864 and treasured his association with the Grand
Army of the Republic for the rest of his life.

In the last days of their lives, after the great-aunts had gone,
picked off one by one like frostbitten chrysanthemums in an autumn garden, after Charlotte had had her heart attack at bridge
club and May had been mugged on Ninth Street on a winter
evening as misty with threat as her own darkening mind, Ruby
and Quint were left alone in the cottage (Roscoe gone long before, killed by a "strangulated hernia," an unnecessary country
ailment).

Ruby had had several heart attacks, her flushed, square face
gone pale ivory afterwards, her bulk not much reduced but with
some of her assurance clipped off; she seemed to be always on the
verge of a question. Quint had a stroke on his ninetieth birthday
but recovered—"A shock like that goes through your whole system," he observed—and lived on and on. He couldn't walk very
well, but he still moved from the living room to the sun parlor to
the dining room, where he had his napkin in the German silver
ring, and sat aristocratic and frail, his starched white shirt holding him up. Finally, he had circulation problems in his legs. Puffing and panting, Ruby lifted him in and out of bed, his leg got
worse, and at last, after an amputation and waking from the anes-
thetic to say, "I've only got one leg now," commenting on his
own history as he was accustomed to do, at the age of ninety-four
he died.

His funeral was conducted in the state that he liked. Ruby
wore black and Mother smoked in the basement. Our Chevy station wagon trailed the hearse up the hill between the banks of
rambler roses to Hankey's Cemetery.

I had come from New York, of course, as soon as I heard that
Grandpa had died, and it interested me to notice that in the two
or three days before the funeral, for the first time in my life I
could remember, my mother and Ruby bickered with each other.
I had always believed Lucille's assertions that she and Ruby had
gotten along perfectly—"Never a cross word"—once she climbed
out of the pit of devastation her father had cast her into by mar-

rying so unexpectedly. Despite beatific references to "my own mother"—the dead Jean—on Lucille's part, and little resentful remarks on Ruby's part about "of *course* you want to go in to see the Girls" (May and Charlotte, that meant) "so you can't spend any time here," Mother and Grandma seemed at one when they were together. Ruby was a bit defensively snobbish ("Well, of course, what was Carrie when she lived over at Aunt Annie's but the maid?") but that was certainly Quint's way too, and Mother and Ruby could chant an antiphonal chorus of gossip, character sketches, tales, and town history over the kitchen sink that sounded rehearsed for generations. During the day or two before we followed Quint's coffin up Hankey's Hill, however, Ruby walked up to me in her living room and said, furious, powder from her large white face speckled over the bosom of her black linen dress, "Your mother smokes all the time and if she doesn't stop, she's going to *die*."

Lucille had not come to be with Ruby from Chautauqua, where she and Chauncey were working as they always did in the summer, until just that week before Quint died. Although she professed the devotion to him she had always showed ("You couldn't get a broomstraw between them"), it was as though at the end she was saying to Ruby, "You wanted him. You took him. Now you have him to care for and bury."

He was gone and Ruby was left alone. She complained in her diary ("Line-A-Day") about being abandoned—"Nobody here but some colored man in a truck asking directions" and "A very, very, lonely day"—but she also wrote down lists of the people from old Parnassus and the countryside around who made the journey out the straight road past the abandoned mine at West's Shaft, past Denny's down at "the corner," up the hill past the mud-colored crumbling stone of Conrad Ludwick's mansion house, and turned into her driveway to condole.

At the end of the summer, a month or two after Grandpa's death, Ruby reluctantly had some of her own antic family to visit. They were reminders of my father's frequently repeated observation that "Ruby didn't come from much." This particular group consisted of a niece, Sis, squat and dark, who had Ruby's coloring and square face but all of it shortened and blurred as in a funhouse mirror; her husband, a lank, stuttering hillbilly with a limp, who was called Hooker because he had once worked as a butcher and "hooked" the meat off the rack; and their adult re- tarded daughter, Pammie, who talked constantly, mouth full or empty but always smeared with lipstick. Sis and her group had come down the river from the wilds of the northwestern part of the state and plunked themselves in the sunporch for a good long three-day gabfest. Ruby had always borne these people with barely contained impatience. Sis, who had the lip-curling snarl of a backwoods bar-and-grill waitress, Ruby could put up with, but Hooker she thought pathetic. And Pammie, she once said to my mother, she simply couldn't stand. (I was shocked; my mother, genuinely liberal, would never have admitted she found Pammie a sight.)

Halfway through Sis's visit, my father in my parents' house in Cedar Hill received a cryptic phone call. "Chauncey?" a woman's voice bleated out of the telephone, "There's somebody wants to talk to you." At which point a high-pitched man's voice cried into Father's ear, "Aunt R's dead."

Making a leap of intuition, Father said incredulously, "You mean Ruby?" and when poor Hooker, into whose shaking hands Sis, a coward after all, had thrust the receiver, said unsteadily, "Yes," Father was told the rest of the story.

Complaining of feeling unwell, Ruby had lain down on the red damask davenport in the living room and simply died.

My mother went up to the country to stay, Sis refusing to be dislodged until the funeral was over, and sat for three days while Sis explained again and again, "I knew she weren't good. I knew she weren't good when she got up that morning, but she made me m'butterscotch pie 'cause that's what I liked and now I don't have the heart to take a mouthful." Indeed, when I got there the day before the funeral, the butterscotch meringue pie sat in the refrigerator in high-peaked splendor, untouched except for one slender sliver. "Who ate a piece?" "I did," said Mother, shrugging. "I got hungry."

"They say she shouldn'ta lived alone. They say she weren't good," stuttered Hooker, eyes wild, head swinging back and forth, and then fearfully, "Mind, I'm just quotin'. I'm just quotin', mind."

Sis went around telling the Parnassus remnant who came to Ruby's funeral that "she died in Hooker's arms and there was nobody she loved more." This was so clearly false that it was met with blank stares, which Sis took for the response appropriate to the Great Blows of Fate.

When I was going through her Line-A-Day diary much later, after my mother had cleaned out the cottage, I saw the entry for the night before Ruby died: *Sis, Hooker, and Pammie here. Guess I'm glad to see them. I feel terrible tonight. I hope I'm not having another heart attack.* The next page was blank.

And that was that. The day after Ruby's funeral there was a cold, early autumn rain and my mother said, standing at her kitchen sink in Cedar Hill, "I can't bear the thought of poor Grandma lying out there in the wet—except"—she caught herself—"of course, it isn't really she—she's in heaven."

I didn't know that for sure, but Mother's certainty seemed to place Ruby there as surely as she and all the Dinsmores—and Ludwicks and Stewarts and Kincaids—had once been placed in Parnassus. What was as sure as their two-hundred-year tenure was that they were there no more. Dead and buried, the culture of that Western Pennsylvania was gone, evanescent as Ruby's spirit, gone from her stout body under the turf of Hankey's Hill.

I went, the next springtime, with my Mother to the old courthouse in the county seat fifteen miles away to witness the closing of the estate.

When Mother and I arrived at the courthouse we checked in with a guard wearing a blue police uniform in a tiled room on the lower floor. Then we took an elevator to an exquisite little courtroom, paneled in dark beveled wood, on an upper floor. A portly, square-jawed old judge passed personal remarks with many of the people appearing before him ("I drove by your place the other day, Ed, and I see that big old oak tree got hit by lightning"), not as though he enjoyed talking to them, but as though he enjoyed the prerogative. Then our lawyer appeared in a side doorway. His name was Stephen Euwer; he was over eighty (the officer who checked us in downstairs had said, "Oh yes, you're here for Steve Euwer, you must be old-timers"). He had taken care of all our family wills and legal dilemmas. He had even once gotten a settlement for Colored Hallie when she fell over a raised-up sidewalk and broke her wrist.

The bailiff announced "The Estate of Ruby B. Dinsmore" and rose to swear Mother in. The bailiff was a vast, frowzy woman, obese in the country way; the layers of fat formed a protection against the specter, if not the fact, of the mines closing or the crops failing. She looked like a caricature of Ruby, who had grown plump in the image, if not the fact, of prosperity.

"Raise your right hand," the bailiff said to Mother.

She intoned, "Do you swear that what you are about to say is the whole truth and only the truth"—she took a breath and then, with a rising voice, "and so shall you swear on That Last Great Day?"

Part Six

POSTLUDE

LUCILLE

1992

"We've lost your mother," said the voice calling from the nursing home.

"Dead?" I said, trying to sound controlled.

"No"—the voice sounded a little desperate—"lost. Gone. She's not here. She didn't sleep in her bed last night. We think she tried to go back to her house."

"It was a whole night before you found this out?"

"No, no"—it was a female voice and now that I had lost control, she assumed a tolerant, faintly amused tone—"she didn't like her roommate, so she asked for blankets and a pillow and said she'd sleep on a lounge chair in the common room. We put her to bed in there, and this morning she was gone."

I put aside the question of why, for $3,500 a month, they had felt free to let her sleep in a chair. "What steps are you taking to find her?" I sounded huffy. I had learned, late in life, that you could usually harness anger and only release it for a full gallop when it suited you; it was a good tactic but, as with many of my perceptions, my performance fell far short of my knowledge, and I could feel the blood surging into my head. "I would like her found in the next hour." I sliced off each word. "As you know, I am a journalist, and I am keeping a record of this. I will have no scruples about taking it to the newspapers." I slammed down the phone.

Unfortunately, the newspapers in Pittsburgh were on strike and had been for months, but nonetheless, I lived in New York and I was going to let them know it.

But where could she be? She was a little frail bundle of bones who had had a massive heart attack two months before and five episodes of congestive heart failure since. Where would an eighty-five-year-old flapper wearing a nightgown embroidered with morning glories go when she left the Christian Center for Senior Care in Cedar Hill, Pennsylvania? I had an image of her hobbling uphill through the suburbs, one slipper off, one slipper on, like Diddle Diddle Dumpling, my son, John, her breath coming faster and shallower as she struggled back to something that was no longer there.

As it turned out, I was right about the slipper, but nothing else. The nurse called back within the hour. "We found her." The nurse's voice was rich with relief, and surprisingly, affection. "She got up to go to the bathroom and she took a wrong turn and ended up sleeping on a couch in the residential wing. She lost a slipper, but she's fine."

"May I speak to her, please?" I lacked the sense of resolution the nurse seemed to have, and I couldn't get out of my snit quite so quickly.

"Hello, sugar bun." Mother's voice, always breathy with the excitement of just being alive, even before that became so precarious, came on the line. "Wasn't that silly? The poor creature in the other bed was making so much noise I just couldn't sleep, so I asked them for a blanket and then when I got up to go to the bathroom, I went through the wrong door. When the nurses found me, they just hugged and hugged me."

Darn tootin' they did.

And within a week the other woman was moved to another room—something I had tried to make happen for a month—leaving Mother in sole soigné command of her territory.

Unfortunately, the space she commanded was bounded by the door of her room opposite the nurses' station.

She couldn't be trusted not to wander again.

This was not the first time in her life that Lucille had been confined. When she was a little girl her mother tied her to the porch railing of their house on Fifth Avenue in Parnassus to punish her. And all her life since, Lucille had been trying to escape the bonds that small spirits imposed. She was wildly curious and hungry for life. She rushed downstairs in the morning in her nightgown to see if the rose tree had bloomed, and she loved little bits of information. "Did you know," she would say, "that in every culture there is a story of a big flood? Now doesn't that just prove that the story of Noah is true?"

She was generous with her enthusiasm. "Peonies have ants on them and you must *always leave them there* because they eat the stickiness that holds the buds closed and if you brush them off, you'll never have any open flowers." She was always the teacher when she wasn't the little girl.

But time and again she had given herself to others and been pulled back from doing what she needed and wanted. Her little sister had died, and she could never be as important as the grief her mother had cherished, and her mother died and her father bound her to him and then cast her off to marry again, and her husband, although handsome and faithful, had lapsed into melancholy soon after their marriage and he was, in any case, as selfish as a dog with a bone. She had wanted to be an actress and her daddy had never let her go, and financially she had rescued him and it was her teacher's retirement investment her husband had drawn out to buy their house, so she was left with almost no retirement money, and she had helped me through years of free-lance vagrancy. And she had done it with grace and style. "It's only money," she would say while buying baked ham for Father's sandwiches and Cheez Whiz for herself. "Hi-ho-the-derry-o, let's live it up," she would say, putting a meat loaf on the table made with hamburger, which she had told Father was round steak ground. The bracelets, the ruffles, the curls, the Cupid's-bow lipstick: She was determined to enjoy herself with the means at hand.

Her authority for cheerfulness was Jesus in one of his dressier images. She would chant, raising her eyebrows meaningfully:

Consider the Lilies of the Field
How they grow.
They toil not, neither do they spin.
Yet Solomon in all his glory
Was not arrayed like one of these.
If God so cares for the grass of the field,
Which today flourishes and tomorrow is cast
into the oven,
How much more will He care for you,
O ye of little faith.

When she was eight-five she had a massive heart attack after a doddering family doctor had told her her shoulder pain was arthritis. She endured as best she could three days of sweating, vomiting, and pain, which she told me on the long-distance telephone was a bad back, perhaps a ruptured disk. But she told her neighbor and friend of forty years, Hat McConnell, that it was her heart. "But what can I do with Chauncey?" she asked.

When she was finally taken to the emergency room, she made jokes, which caused them to classify her as disoriented.

"This will kill *me*," Chauncey said of Lucille's heart attack. "You've been a wonderful son," he told me, "and Mother's been a wonderful wife, but this will kill me." Arguably, I told him, it would kill Mother.

Then began a terrible time. One evening when she had been released to the CCSC and I had come to visit her there, I walked into her room to find her gray in the face, sweating, and heaving for breath, still dressed in the flowered skirt and shoulder scarf she had put on for my visit. "I'm having a bad spell," she told me, the locket made from her father's ruby ring winking on her breastbone as it rose and fell with each hard-won breath.

"D'you hear that rattle?" she said. In her throat an ominous knocking announced itself from the Beyond.

"Hang on," I said, holding her hand. "I will," she answered as her eyelids drooped. And then, taking one rasping gasp, she clenched her jaw and said, "*I will.*"

And by the time the medics came, her breathing was easier.

After that she announced from her hospital bed that something had to be done. "This could kill a person," she said. There was surgery and a heavy regimen of medication, and she began slowly to mend. Her mind was cloudy from time to time—"Insufficient blood to the brain," said the doctor. "Irreversible." It was then that she wandered away on her odyssey to the other wing.

My fantasy of her running away altogether from the Christian Center for Senior Care and trailing through the hilly streets of town in her nightgown with the hollyhocks owed something certainly to my bred-in-the-bone memory of the tale of Massy Harbison. Like the primeval heroine, Lucille had made a trek through the wilderness, only in Lucille's case it was the wilderness of adversity. Attacked by brutal forces beyond her control, seeing loved ones felled on every side, reviled and neglected by those who had made themselves her keepers, who could say whether this described capture by Indians in the eighteenth century or old age in the twentieth?

And the captivity narrative—that indigenous subgenre of American literature that begins with the first accounts of the first captives taken away from the chaste and chilly pleasures of Olde New England to live quite happily in some cases (once they got there) with savage red spouses who gamboled like children in their woodland homes—that narrative that combined the lure of the exotic with the threat of the possible, it too had its analogue in the Christian Center for Senior Care. "Everyone is so good to me here," my mother would say.

"Too my surprize nobodye doeth mee harm and I be well fad as att my Father's tabel in Braintree," ran an old chronicle.

No matter how pleasant a captive's time may have been, the Job's Comforters at home refused to believe it, of course. "How brave you've been. I just think it's marvelous, when you had to leave your little home and all," wrote Mother's lifelong school friend and rival Naomi Vogel Russell, with whom she had entered into the truce of extreme old age. "Little home indeed!" snorted Mother.

But irreversibly there was the captivity. Mother improved in health more than anyone could have predicted. She graduated backwards in a manner almost unknown in nursing homes, from the floor where they moaned in their beds to a floor where only a few were bedridden to a wing where little boxy rooms held memento-choked bureaus and a chair beside the bed from which the ladies rose from afternoon naps and forayed down to dinner. The confinement of Lucille to her chair on the nursing floor had been of short duration, no bands of winding sheet though perhaps a presage of that inevitable swaddling. Contrary to the doctor's grim prognostication, her mind cleared except for some trouble with proper names at which she made approximate jabs. We fixed up a suite for her and Father, a charming living room and bedroom looking out onto a pear tree and a hillside covered with trees. It was furnished with things from home—Father's big red leather rocking chair with the swans' heads on the arms, marble-top tables from Parnassus—and it was as pleasant as pleasant could be. In captivity.

"Darling, the truth of the matter is that I don't know *anyone* who wouldn't rather be ten years younger and living on their own," Lucille said to Chauncey in answer to the interminable rolling river of his complaints. But they weren't on their own.

Sadly enough, after all those years they weren't really together either, in spirit, at least. When Lucille had first gone to the nursing home there was no room for Chauncey, and he had been left at home with so-called caregivers whose faces and food were as gray as Mrs. Gummidge. Father's complaint of "The meat's tough" gave way to "The meat's gummy." The women showed up on time, they cooked after a fashion, and they didn't steal anything—otherwise they were useless. One night Father fell—he had the beginnings of Parkinson's disease and was unsteady on his feet. The woman present looked at him on the floor and said, "I can't help you. I have a bad back." He was ninety-three at the time. He got himself up.

But by the end of the summer when the suite had become available at the CCSC, Chauncey had adjusted to being alone with the caregivers. Lucille, free for the first time in more than fifty years from cajoling, amusing, turning haughty on Chauncey (she ignored him emotionally and pampered him physically when she couldn't deal with him—the worst combination for a melancholiac), was like a little girl on vacation with elderly relations. "That peach belongs to *me*," she said proudly, pointing to a peach on her dresser when she was still sharing a room in the nursing wing. She submitted to bingo, tabletop bowling, the indignities of knocking pieces of wood together during the rhythm band at Sing-Along. "This is an *adventure*," she said, using her old code for something quite disagreeable that she was determined to endure with style.

So when they came together again, Chauncey and Lucille, he behaved badly. He was resentful about losing his home, about losing his privacy, about being *old*. He spat on the floor in the corridors (his throat was stiff but his manners had always been so nice), and he blamed Lucille for their being there. Each of them thought they were in the CCSC because of the other. He was getting along perfectly fine with the caregivers, he said. "I missed Mother, but I would rather things had stayed the way they were."

"I could have gone to Friendly Village with all those teachers," she said. "But we needed to be here so they could give Daddy his medicine and help him bathe."

He hounded her and badgered her. "I've heard him. He just never lets up," the head nurse told me, her cap bristling with indignation.

He wore her down. "Make it do, wear it out, use it up. That's what they say in Boston," she said. "And that's what I feel like."

"How do you like the center, Mr. Kincaid?" visitors would ask politely. "Well, if you want to live in a chicken coop with no privacy, I suppose it's all right." He was uncompromising.

"I don't think you love me anymore," Lucille said.

"I couldn't live without you," Chauncey answered as though she were a portable oxygen tank.

"Wasn't that nice of him?" my mother said.

And so, there they were left. Quint was gone. Ruby was gone. Jane Hamilton was gone, dead after six months of a wasting cancer in the nursing wing of St. George's, the home where I had learned about the ankle bracelet years ago. Charlotte was gone. May was gone. Parnassus was gone, finally. Its name having been taken away sixty years before when it was consolidated with New Kensington, it had now decayed into a slum, the big old wooden houses partly veneered in garish sidings of purple, sky blue, and dirty pink, when I made the pilgrimage up the river one afternoon and drove through town under a lurid, thundery sky. There was a heap of slag in the corner of the Parnassus Presbyterian Church yard, a remnant of the long-dead mines, trucked from some skeletal shaft out the creek road and dumped once, dead as yesterday's hope, to make a drive for nobody. A young woman with tangled hair and two men wearing leather vests with tattoos on their bare arms leaned against a motorcycle in front of Charlotte and May's house. One of the big old trees on Fifth Avenue, farther up the street, was dead.

It was not all of America, but it was a part of America that had been there from the beginning. The men had done it; they had come to the wilderness with hope that was richly satisfied, and then the women, bearing more men and women, had kept life alive until, in the end, the women in their strength were left with men who had no life. All of them had done the best they knew—and they studied so as to know. The Westminster Catechism ("What is the Chief End of Man? A. To Glorify God and Enjoy Him Forever" is the first question there), the Bible, the Carnegie Library—giving back something to the Pennsylvania hills from which old Andrew's money had come—all of it was a way to talk and a way to think for the people in those hills and valleys. Two hundred years ago they had come there because it was as far as they could go. And now they had gone as far as they could.

In the Name of God Amen. I Conrad Ludwick of Franklin Township Do make, constitute and ordain this my last Will and Testament in the name and form following: . . . I will and bequeath to my beloved wife Mary over and above other bequests hereafter mentioned the sole use and possession of the new house, situate over the run from the Old Mansion House and also the privilege of using the Spring, Springhouse and the cellar during her natural life, also I bequeath to my beloved wife Mary the one third part of the live stock, all her wearing apparel, bed and bedding, a table, her saddle and all the kitchen furniture.

$\mathcal{A}$cknowledgments

Among the many, many people who have listened to me tell these stories and who have encouraged me to complete the book I must particularly mention Margaretta Barton Colt, who understands where the stories come from; Constance Sullivan, who has been supportive through many revisions; Jack L. Goldstein, who could practically retell the stories by heart; and the Walton sisters, whose appreciation of the setting and whose humor and love left their descendant rich in love.

Thomas Mallon read the manuscript and made sensitive criticisms at an early stage.

I would like to thank Paige Rense for her professional generosity in putting me in touch with the late Leo Lerman and his companion, Gray Foy, who helped to shape the manuscript at a crucial point.

My agent, Wendy Weil, stuck with the manuscript and me through several stages in the pre-publication days.

And finally I can only be wonderfully grateful for the intelligence, imagination, and patience of my editor, Peter Borland.